Organizational DNA

Organizational DNA

**Diagnosing
Your
Organization
for
Increased
Effectiveness**

Linda Honold and
Robert J. Silverman

DAVIES-BLACK PUBLISHING

Palo Alto, California

Published by Davies-Black Publishing, a division of CPP, Inc., 3803 East Bayshore Road, Palo Alto, CA 94303; 800-624-1765.

Special discounts on bulk quantities of Davies-Black books are available to corporations, professional associations, and other organizations. For details, contact the Director of Book Marketing and Sales at Davies-Black Publishing, 3803 East Bayshore Road, Palo Alto, CA 94303; 650-691-9123; fax 650-623-9271.

Visit the Davies-Black Publishing Web site at www.daviesblack.com.

Printed in the United States of America
06 05 04 03 02   10 9 8 7 6 5 4 3 2 1

Library of Congress Cataloging-in-Publication Data
Honold, Linda
    Organizational DNA: diagnosing your organization for increased effectiveness /
    Linda Honold and Robert J. Silverman.— 1st ed.
        p. cm.
    Includes bibliographical references and index.
    ISBN 0-89106-175-4
        1. Organizational effectiveness. 2. Leadership. 3. Management.
        4. Organizational effectiveness—Case studies. I. Silverman, Robert J.
        (Robert Jay). II. Title.

    HD58.9 .H655 2002
    658.4′01—dc21   2002034974

FIRST EDITION
First printing 2002

Contents

Preface

As DNA is the genetic building block of life, so "organizational DNA" is the foundation for effective leadership and management. In this book we argue that organizations manifest four primary types of organizational DNA and require alignment between their basic identity and their leadership and management practices.

Following descriptions and origins of the concept of organizational DNA, in part 1 we introduce four organizations, each exemplifying one of the four DNA types, to demonstrate how a specific DNA type leads to variations in the same organizational practices. In part 2 we examine the consequences of appropriate and inappropriate alignments of organizational practices with the different DNA types. Discussed are methods for attaining alignment, current leadership and management issues, and the implications of considering DNA in relation to these issues. Additionally, a diagnostic tool is provided to help you determine your organization's DNA.

We invite you to think about your organization's practices and programs for improvement—those that worked and those that did not. It is our expectation that you will find that what worked did so because it matched your organization's DNA and that what did not work reflected another DNA type.

Linda Honold
Milwaukee, WI

Robert J. Silverman
Vancouver, WA

Acknowledgments

It would have been impossible to write this book without the assistance of many people. I most especially wish to acknowledge those who work at the organizations presented here as exemplars of the four DNA types. To the employees of Springfield Remanufacturing, Johnsonville Sausage, YSI, and Wainwright Industries, thank you for sharing with me the story of your company. I would also like to acknowledge the people working in the dozens of organizations I have consulted with over the past fifteen years whose experiences have also supported the concepts presented.

I'd like to thank my coauthor, Robert J. Silverman, who served as chair of my dissertation committee at the Fielding Graduate Institute, for his insight into organizations and overview of the literature and their application to the companies that I studied.

Finally, I'd like to express my appreciation for the support and validation I receive almost daily from my husband, Reynolds, and my daughter, Samantha.

Linda Honold

Each of us can identify important teachers who helped us to ask the right questions and who provided guidance as we grappled with those questions—and who were models of excellence and integrity. For me this includes Francis Fergusson at Rutgers; Philip Phenix at Teachers College, Columbia; Gerald Gordon, William Foote Whyte, and Isabel Peard at Cornell; and Esther Hawkins in an earlier stage of learning. I am indebted to each, as I am to Arliss L. Roaden, who brought me to Ohio State as a faculty member and whose support allowed a twenty-four-year editorship at the *Journal of Higher Education*, where I worked alongside excellence in many written forms. I also wish to thank Eleanor Scott Meyers, former dean of the Human and Organization Development Program at the Fielding Graduate Institute, who placed me among extraordinary student and faculty colleagues.

To my family, I owe the most important understanding of what appears here. I dedicate this book to my children, Rachael, David, and Alana—who exemplify how commitments based on personal integrity grounded in hope and justice can serve the larger good through very different journeys—and to my wife, Maxine, a person who combines caring, commitment, competence, and, most especially, love for her family.

Robert J. Silverman

Introduction

Why is cultural change so difficult to achieve in organizations? Why is it that organizational improvement efforts that are so successful for some are such dismal failures for others? Why do effective approaches to the development of a mission, governance structure, and leadership vary so much from company to company? Why does teamwork work for one company and not for another? It is our contention that these and similar questions can be answered by understanding a core component that defines almost every aspect of organizations: *organizational DNA*.

THE BASIC CONCEPT OF ORGANIZATIONAL DNA

Organizational DNA represents a deliberate way of thinking about organizations and their patterns and about leadership and management practices within their related contexts. As the foundation for understanding organizations, it replaces many alternative approaches that address organizational models or forms—and such practices as teamwork, decision making, and employee development—as separate, or at least more independent, considerations and activities.

Organizational DNA has its roots in early Western thought, reflected in writings and practices over many centuries. The application here allows us to consider organizations as comprising four distinct types related to the everyday work world:

◊ *Factual DNA:* linear models and calculations

◊ *Conceptual DNA:* theories, paradigms, and overriding concepts

◊ *Contextual DNA:* relationships in internal and external environments

◊ *Individual DNA:* individuals, either alone or with others

Factual DNA speaks to the reality of our factual world and to organizations that are committed to knowing themselves and their environments through the collection of data. This information provides a constant barometer and continual assessment of performance. It is also crucial in the development of all policies and procedures.

Conceptual DNA focuses on large motivating ideas that may take the form of major theories, visions, and other conceptual devices. We use these ideas to orient ourselves to belief systems, ideologies, and frameworks that often provide justification and guidance to our life and work.

Contextual DNA deals with the environments in which we function. It directs our attention to the problems and issues we face and the strategies we employ as we shape our organizations and the contexts in which they are situated in relation to each other.

And, individual DNA is about us as individuals, people who live in cooperation with each other but also singularly, with our own voices, wills, goals, and interests. In human terms, we are inventive as we develop positive, appreciative, relationships within our organizations that will sustain us in the fulfillment of our deeper needs.

Each DNA type leads to different attitudes and practices: the factual to estimating, predicting, and figuring; the conceptual to believing, contending, denying, and presuming; the contextual to discovering, learning, perceiving, and relating; and the individual to desiring, fearing, hoping, and preferring.

Dominant DNA

Each organization finds itself located primarily in one of the DNA types. Yet, as described later, all four DNA types have a presence in each of the others, but they are defined differently within each primary, dominant type. We assert, for example, that should a factual-based organization attempt to implement an improvement effort in the same way as an individual-based company, it likely will not succeed; that the governance structure in a conceptual-based company is quite different from one based on individual relationships; and that teams in a contextual-based organization are developed and implemented differently than they would be in a factual-based organization.

Each of the organizational DNA types, then, reflects different definitions for similar practices and different ways of thinking. It is not unlike individuals of different faiths engaged in similar practices—such as reading holy texts, praying, being involved in life-cycle events—but bringing different meanings to them. These religious practices each have integrity within their specific faiths and could not be transposed to others. This book is about the integrity we believe is essential for successful organizational functioning.

THE MODEL AND ITS FOUNDATIONS

We developed the model at work some years ago while looking at a particular issue that we felt needed fresh attention, namely, ethical practices associated with research activities within different academic cultures. We were concerned with how scholars related to each other as peers. Just as there are different kinds of organizations, there are different kinds of peer academic communities, where the norms relating to how individuals might more effectively relate to their work and to each other need to be different for good research and professional relationships to be realized.

The problem was that these differences were not broadly understood; research oversight seemed to be based solely on the norms of a fact-oriented culture. As we examined and categorized the communities and ethical practices related to them, we identified the four dimensions described above. We inadvertently discovered that many other researchers had developed models reflecting the four DNA types that were similar or complementary to our own. These included, for example,

◊ The functioning of organizations to include such areas as trust, organizational learning, and leadership

◊ A variety of ethics as expressed in various social institutions, from religion to business

◊ Complex topics such as anatomical medical interventions, forms of higher education and curricula, approaches to action research, and the roles of editors of print and electronic publications

You would think that each scholar who used what we are labeling the organizational DNA model would understand that others had identified the same dimensions that they had presented in line with their focused topics. Interestingly, this was not the case. Each author typically worked in his or her silo, whether it was a field of study or a professional venue, and was unaware of the contributions of others outside his or her usual frame of reference. While we have collected literally scores of treatments either based on or identifying the same four types, we have seen few treatments that acknowledged any others.

This led us to question whether there was a foundation that informed the treatments we were constantly discovering. Indeed, our investigations led us to philosophical foundations as far back as ancient Greece and Rome (McKeon 1994; Pepper 1942). It is not surprising that a conceptual model that we find reinvented in scores of scholarly and professional situations should have a base in the foundations of our culture and, except for philosophical works, be largely unspoken.

In our research, we discovered that the four dimensions in our model were also present in numerous organizational frameworks, though each framework was labeled differently. Fuchs (1992), Adler and Borys (1996), and Quinn and Cameron (1999), for example, each with synoptic perspectives, posit models containing four variations that are complementary to our model. Quinn and Cameron's work on organizational culture, for instance, denotes such alternatives as a hierarchy culture and a clan culture, among others, which are compatible with our factual and individual DNA–based types. We mention these resources to encourage our readers to engage this additional material and to suggest the universality of what we present: our model is centrally embedded in the logic of our culture.

DISCERNING YOUR ORGANIZATION'S DNA

For this concept to be useful, you must be able to discern your organization's DNA type. As we will see, this understanding is critical for undertaking resolution of organizational problems, as well as in selecting the appropriate consultants and other resources for organizational improvement.

We ask that you act as a participant-observer in your organizational setting, reflecting on what you experience and attempting to make sense of it in terms of the DNA model outlined in this book. Although this might take some getting used to, you must be engaged in the action around you and, at the same time, stand outside of it. Try to understand the meaning of what you are experiencing and ask yourself: (1) What does this reveal about the deeper or hidden DNA of the organization? and (2) What does this reveal about how individuals in the organization think about and make sense of everyday activities?

By looking at your organizational practices carefully and considering their DNA alignment, you will be able not only to discern your DNA, but also to develop your organization in the most effective manner. You will be able to do this by engaging in relevant leadership and management practices and through seeking appropriate consultation around interventions that will enhance current organizational alignments.

Synopsis of DNA Types in Four Organizations

What do organizations exemplifying each of the four types of DNA look like? In the late nineties Honold (1998, 1999) studied four organizations identified as "empowering." At the time of her study each had been using empowering practices for more than fifteen years. She found that, contrary to what might have been expected in four organizations practicing a common concept, the management practices in these organizations had few similarities. For instance, two used teams extensively; one used them only on rare occasions; one did not use them at all. Hiring practices were vastly different. The use, even the existence, of a mission, vision, or value statement varied in each company's approach and development.

Each of the four companies examined is manufacturing based and relatively small (under 1,250 employees). Since the time of the study, all four have undoubtedly moved beyond the practices described here, as they are dynamic organizations, and change in this environment happens very quickly. Despite these limitations, an examination of their approaches to management provides a classic example of the differences experienced due to varying types of DNA. And, while each firm is examined in the context of its dominant DNA type, it must be remembered that each has the other types in evidence, as described in later chapters.

Obviously there are facts, concepts, contexts, and individuals in every organization, regardless of DNA type. However, each specific DNA type defines and interprets the meaning of those categories in systematically different ways. We will see, for example, that the significance of factual material in a conceptual DNA–based organization is quite different from what it is in an individual DNA–based organization. And the same is true for each of the other possible connections between types, as the unfolding stories will make evident.

Factual DNA:
Springfield Remanufacturing
Corporation

Springfield Remanufacturing Corporation (SRC) rebuilds diesel motors, alternators, and fuel injection systems among other engine parts. It also runs additional businesses, including a machine shop and a business devoted to delivering seminar, consulting, and publishing products. In over fifteen years, this employee-owned enterprise has spun off fifteen businesses in all.

Years ago, while developing their work processes, management realized that the more information they provided employees with, the more innovative and entrepreneurial the employees became. Management believed that the source of the company's growth was each employee's focus on the bottom line and his or her understanding of the profit-and-loss statement. Case (1993) has called SRC a company of business people, and it prides itself on its employees' entrepreneurial style.

THE MANAGEMENT PROCESS

The management process is actually a series of tightly interrelated communication processes that help all organizational participants focus on a common goal: the company's financial results. This process is repetitive; it is the mechanism by which the company is managed year in and year out.

The process begins with the setting of annual projections. These are introduced at a meeting between the sales/marketing and management staffs of the various divisions. The managers from each area, in turn, share the tentative plans with their staffs. Supervisors take their portion of the plan and communicate it to the production workers, who determine whether or not they can produce what has been forecast. A support staff including the supervisor, the division accountant, materials purchasers, and engineers provides the production staff with technical advice to assist them in determining their ability to do the work.

The production plan is then returned to the facility's management to determine its economic feasibility. Adjustments are made if needed, and the plan is then returned to production. When agreement is attained, the plan is adopted. It becomes the formalized projection document to which actual performance will be compared during the next fiscal year.

The next step in the process is to determine what SRC labels the "critical numbers." Critical numbers are measurements, such as profit before tax, that lead to improvement over the previous year's results. They serve as a form of insurance policy to help offset a perceived weakness in the company.

Actual performance is compared to both the critical numbers and the profit-and-loss statement and shared with all members of the organization through a series of weekly meetings called "huddles" (Stack 1992) or staff meetings. The staff meeting process begins with the frontline worker tracking his or her own production. Supervisors aggregate each work unit's production numbers onto the modified profit-and-loss statement and report the unit numbers to the production manager. On Monday or Tuesday of each week facility management team members, including the general manager, sales manager, accountant, production manager, purchasing/materials manager, and engineer, report the data from their areas of responsibility at a pre–staff meeting that lasts from sixty to ninety minutes. A member of the financial division enters the data, and the statement is then reviewed by the entire group to develop an understanding of, and a plan to deal with, any discrepancies from the facility's original plan.

The corporate staff meeting takes place every other Wednesday morning. In attendance are all corporate staff, the general manager of each division, and other divisional members, as needed, to provide input or at their request. Generally fifty to sixty people are present. The meeting has two parts.

The first part is similar to the pre–staff meeting. Each line of the profit-and-loss statement is filled in for each company. With a laptop computer, a spreadsheet program, and a data projector, this financial information is projected in spreadsheet form onto a large screen for all to see. Each line is highlighted and, as the cursor moves to each unit of the organization, the manager responsible for that area calls out the number. Any discrepancy of ±5 percent from the plan must be explained and requires that a plan be presented to get back on track. It is just as important to explain "performance better than planned" as "performance worse than planned." The goal is to be on target: no better, no worse.

The second part of the corporate staff meeting is social in nature. Company announcements about special events are made, as are personal announcements such as the birth of employees' children, and there are celebrations in response to certifications of professional development. If a customer has visited a division, this fact is announced to all. Since many of the companies share customers, they may find ways to bring the customer to other sites as well.

At the end of the meeting, the spreadsheet is saved, printed, and immediately distributed to attendees. Every other week, when there is no staff meeting, numbers are faxed to corporate headquarters, collated by staff, and returned via fax to all divisions.

Post–staff meetings are held within forty-eight hours of the corporate staff meeting. Managers have meetings with their staff members and relate what happened at the corporate staff meeting. The supervisors then have meetings with department production members to share the information. These meetings, generally lasting twenty to thirty minutes, have opening phases that are generally educational, in which the division accountant leads a practical discussion regarding an aspect of the financial statement.

The internal audit is the final phase of the weekly staff meeting process. On Friday, a person from Human Resources goes to each group to ask individuals whether they had their weekly post–staff meeting and to determine if they know their unit's performance in comparison to the sales goals and critical numbers. The internal audit serves to reinforce managers' sharing information with all members of the organization. With the conclusion of the audit, the weekly cycle is complete and ready to begin again on Monday morning.

The management system is repeated on an annual basis—last year's results lead to the development of new critical numbers to sales and projection forecasts and then to budgets. Once this is all set, the process of weekly meetings begins anew. The rules do not change. Everything is the same, so employees know what to count on from week to week, from month to month, and from year to year.

HISTORICAL PERSPECTIVE

It is important to understand the history of the company to appreciate why this system was developed. SRC was originally part of International Harvester, which in the early 1980s was downsizing (from 110,000 to 15,000 employees worldwide in just two years). Employees at the plant were asking management if their jobs were going to be eliminated. Plant management did not know the answer; they were subject to decisions made at corporate headquarters over 500 miles away.

Faced with the probability of having to close the factory, several members of the plant's management opted to attempt to purchase the facility. Financial institutions, however, were not anxious to take on such a risky venture. The managers grew increasingly angry as financial institutions turned them down, one after another. In the course of this process, the managers realized that they did not know enough about financial management to run a company well. Thus, once the loan was finally obtained, they set out to build the company, now highly leveraged, with employees who understood financial management, believing that this would help keep the company in good financial shape.

GOVERNANCE STRUCTURE

Overall, the company structure is similar to most business hierarchies. There are traditional executive and managerial functions. Supervisors are in place in each area, but there are few layers of management. Production employees who want to speak to the general manager of their division must pass through two levels; there are two additional levels to reach the CEO. Despite the hierarchy, communications are free-flowing. Anyone may talk to anyone else at any point, although it is considered common courtesy to let the immediate supervisor know that this is happening.

BUSINESS EDUCATION

Business education is taken very seriously in the company. While it doesn't cost a great deal of money to get individuals engaged and to have them understand what falls to the bottom line, it does take a bit of creative thinking on the managers' part. For instance, one of the facilities had an opportunity to significantly reduce insurance costs if it improved safety. Plant management came up with the idea that if it achieved 1 million safe hours, the male production foreman would put on a dress and parade around the plant. The novelty of the incentive, however comical, worked, and it saved the facility hundreds of thousands of dollars.

In addition to a new-employee orientation, there is a career-planning program. The company provides opportunities for growth, and it is mandatory that all employees participate in career planning. Each year, every employee looks at annual and longer-term goals and develops plans to achieve them. Not everyone wants to become a leader, so skill enhancement opportunities are made available. Reimbursement is also made available for formal educational programs.

COMMUNITY INVOLVEMENT

SRC uses community involvement not only as a way to provide a service, but also as a way to educate workers. One program brought third graders into the workplace to teach them about jobs in the factory, with factory workers serving as trainers. The company created an additional program through which the young students ran a miniature business selling pen, pencil, and ruler sets.

PERSONAL RESPONSIBILITY

Part of the education process is to have individuals take responsibility for dealing with their own work issues. Production workers are continually trying to find ways to reduce their production costs. They can implement ideas on their own. If other departments will be affected, or if parts need to be purchased, a supervisor will act as a facilitator. If the issue is one of great magnitude, those involved will call on management for assistance.

Employees are expected to deal with most problems they encounter, and new employees are expected to enter the process fairly quickly. They are immediately initiated to two main rules: (1) don't get hurt, and (2) if you don't know what you're supposed to be doing, ask somebody.

When other departments or other facilities are struggling, the idea is to help them succeed. For instance, an advisory team may be formed to assist facilities having difficulty getting their costs under control or with meeting product-shipping schedules. The team becomes a champion for that business, getting them to move in the right direction.

FINANCIAL REWARDS

The final element of this tightly woven operation is a rewards system. Rewards take several forms including base wage, the employee stock ownership program (ESOP), and the bonus system.

The base wage system is traditional, with employees being paid based on the job that they do. The ESOP and the bonus system are new. While employees may not join the company for the ESOP, they quickly see it as important as they begin owning stock in the company. Every employee who has been at the company for more than a year becomes a part of the ESOP.

The bonus system is basically the same for everyone in the company. Bonuses are paid out quarterly based on the achievement of the facility's critical numbers. Since each plant sets its own critical numbers, bonuses are based on different criteria.

Each facility has some flexibility in its reward policies. One unit provides a monthly bonus payout on issues that are causing them difficulty, such as safety or accuracy: regardless of financial performance, all employees receive an extra $25 each month if the goal is met. Another facility has experimented with a pay-for-skill system in which employees are compensated for each additional skill set they learn and apply.

SUMMARY

The system of work at SRC has virtually every person in the company becoming a manager of his or her own work. The interlocking staff meeting process involves every employee in the financial results of the company on a weekly basis. Financially focused education backs up the system. Compensation reinforces the achievement of fact-based goals. When individuals, departments, or plants are having performance difficulty, peer pressure may be applied through public pronouncements regarding such difficulties at a staff meeting. However, colleagues will also band together to assist those in trouble get back on track by creating a team champion—ultimately, if one plant fails, it affects all the employee-owners.

Dominant at Springfield Remanufacturing is factual DNA: the focus is on the balance sheet. As stated earlier, all the other types of DNA—conceptual, contextual, and individual—are present in this organization, but they are defined and interpreted by the dominant factual DNA in systematically different ways. The conceptual DNA–based component is exemplified by the use of capitalism as the primary driving idea, including the spinning-off of companies to exploit opportunities to generate additional revenue. Contextual DNA is manifested in the weekly staff meetings to keep the focus on the balance sheet. Individual DNA is represented through a rational system: the employee stock option program. These subsidiary types look quite different at organizations grounded in a different dominant DNA type.

Conceptual DNA:
Johnsonville Sausage

Johnsonville Sausage in Sheboygan Falls, Wisconsin, has been working with its approach to empowerment since 1982. In 1988 Tom Peters described management at Johnsonville as having "gone the furthest of anyone anywhere at handing the reins of control to the workers" (Peters 1988). Since then, the process has evolved through several iterations.

PHASE 1: ORGANIZATIONAL EVOLUTION

Prior to its current organizational philosophy, the company's owners were in firm and total control. They determined what was to be done, how it would be done, who would do what, and when they would do it. The single goal was to "sell high-quality sausage and make money doing it." Then, in 1978, the founder's son, Ralph C. Stayer, became president. Through his involvement with groups such as the Young

Presidents Organization and The Executive Committee, he developed a different set of directives for an ideal organization:

◊ Have everyone be totally responsible for his or her own performance

◊ Have a common focus of where the company is going—every person must work together with others, doing whatever it takes to reach their common goal

◊ Be perfectly designed for the task at hand

◊ Be flexible enough to change work group formations and alliances to fit the task at hand

◊ Be structured such that people can learn from one another

In initiating this change, Stayer and his executive committee first developed a company mission statement. It focused on the company becoming customer oriented and on getting every worker to commit to the common goal and to be responsible for his or her performance. It suggested that as the company became more customer focused, change would be a constant. This document became the guiding light for changing the company. At the beginning, however, the specifics of the mission statement were not shared with others.

Stayer initially met with the employees in groups of four, in what became known as "four-on-ones." He explained his vision about personal responsibility and that if they noticed a problem with the product they should get it fixed, even if it meant shutting down the assembly line.

Formation of Teams

Several cross-functional teams were formed, including the Company Performance Share team. This group was charged with determining how the company could share profits with all employees while at the same time accounting for performance. The team was composed of individuals who would be receiving the profits: employees and leadership. While two executive team members served as advisors to the group, the owner directed the parameters within which this team would operate: (1) the amount of profits to be shared would be determined by the executives; (2) the money would not be shared across the board, based on seniority, or based on a percentage of a person's current wage; and (3) the money would be shared based somehow on performance. The team then determined a way to share the money available.

Other Changes

Management created a yearly $100 Personal Development Fund that could be spent on anything an employee chose, as long as he or she would learn from it. The learning did not need to be work related—it was believed that once an employee began learning, the process would have a positive effect on his or her performance.

Senior management changed the base pay system from across-the-board increases to increases based only on additional responsibility. If a sausage stuffer took on responsibility for keeping an inventory track of product casings, that individual would have increased value to the company such that they would not have to hire an additional worker to perform that function. In this win-win scenario, the company receives additional value, and the employee receives additional compensation.

Titles were changed to reflect responsibilities held. Executives became "resource team members," managers became "coordinators," supervisors became "coaches," and employees became "members." Individuals were involved in changes to their work area. For instance, instead of a plant engineer alone determining how to lay out a new production line, he or she would involve those who would actually be working on that line. The engineer would then incorporate their ideas into the implementation plan.

PHASE 2: SHIFTING RESPONSIBILITY AND INDIVIDUAL LEARNING

Phase 2 began with a two-pronged approach: a focus on changing systems in order to shift responsibility and a focus on learning. Both were accomplished simultaneously.

Shifting Responsibility

The Johnsonville vision of the ideal workforce was for individuals to take responsibility for their own performance. To achieve that sense of responsibility, each worker would have input into work details. The manager would continue to set the big picture, indicating *what* must be accomplished. The worker would have input into *how* he or she would get the job done. The system was therefore changed so that the primary responsibility for budgeting would be in the workers' hands.

Johnsonville management discovered that raw material costs were way out of line with what they should be. Upon further investigation, they found that the main culprits were scrap and poor-quality products. The management team looked at the issue strategically. Instead of making quick fixes to bring costs in line, they developed a four-year action plan to change the budgeting system. The result was that the responsibility for controlling the cost of raw materials was placed with those on the front line.

In the first year, the accountants worked with plant management to develop a budget based on raw materials, labor, and overhead costs as well as sales projections for each product. The accountants then provided plant management with monthly reports on exact performance numbers. In the second year, the frontline coaches were involved in the same process, and in the third year members of the frontline work team were brought in. As the frontline people became familiar with the budget, they were able to make suggestions for improvement in the production process, resulting in decreased costs. Management was no longer instructing them what to do. Rather, a system was put in place so that the performers could determine how they could meet the goals that had been mutually set in the budgeting process.

The customer complaint process was redesigned to transfer responsibility to the workers. The customer service department was transformed into a clearinghouse. When a complaint was called in, the customer service representative would take down the pertinent information and would tell the customer that he or she would be called back with an indication of how the issue would be resolved.

The customer service representative then transmitted the information to the appropriate department, which then identified someone from the department to take responsibility for investigating the issue and getting back to the customer with an explanation of what had occurred and how the company would make sure it never happened again. Workers began to take control of problematic situations by addressing issues as they came up instead of waiting until they returned as customer complaints.

Individual Learning

The organization was changing. Employees were taking more responsibility. This had never been expected of them in the past, but it needed to be developed. The company needed individuals who were open to change. Management, acknowledging the reciprocal relationship between change and learning, assumed that individuals who were learning would be more open to change. As a result, the focus on individual learning became the second prong of this phase of organizational change. (For information on specific learning resources, see appendix 2.)

Following are some examples of learning opportunities created by the personal development team, which consisted of members from throughout the organization.

◊ The Personal Development Workshop helped individuals assess their learning styles, values, and personal constraints as well as inventory their current skills and those they would like to acquire, for which they would create a learning contract.

◊ The Continuing Education Program provided assistance with tuition, should the development plan include a formal education component.

◊ The Member Interaction Program gave every organizational member the opportunity to spend a day working with any other member. For instance, after spending a day with a salesperson, individual members in Manufacturing or in Billing could begin to see how what they did affected Sales. They realized their work had a direct impact on the customer, and their jobs began to take on a whole new meaning.

◊ The "Intrapreneurship" was designed to allow organizational members the opportunity to run their own business with support from the larger company. For example, an accounts payable clerk had an idea for establishing a mail-order department. She had internal support and assistance but was also free to purchase from outside the company. She had bottom-line profit responsibility for the performance of the mail-order department. After a couple of years of running the business as the first "Intrapreneur," she moved on to a new challenge and a new member took over the mail-order department, thus enabling the learning process to continue.

Institutionalizing the Mission

In 1987 the resource team sent out a copy of the mission statement. Small group meetings were held to discuss its meaning. People were asked to provide ideas on how the mission could be met in their work areas. Work groups began to have regular meetings to keep focused on the common goal and on their part in reaching that goal.

PHASE 3: THE SUMMIT CONFERENCE

By 1991 Johnsonville had reached a plateau. It needed something to rekindle change and to continue the process of transferring responsibility. The president called a company-wide meeting—a summit conference, as it was known—to address the issue. Any company member interested in attending was invited, as the conference was to be held on a Saturday and Sunday, and management stressed that this meeting would determine where the company was going and how it was going to get there. Though attendance was not mandatory, about 120 of the company's approximately 750 employees—including managers, coaches, resource or support personnel, and production employees—chose to attend.

Revisiting Company Goals

The first order of business at the off-site conference was to revisit the company's goals: Where was it going? Who were the customers? What were the critical success measures? The meeting participants developed four key areas that would become the "Four Ideal End States," providing the foci of all activities throughout the company: (1) make products that are consistently the best; (2) provide service that contributes to the success of the customers; (3) have financial results that are noticeably better than the competition's; and (4) provide the best place to work for those who have chosen to be a part of the company.

Of these, only financial results had specific targets defined by the company owners. Financial results are the prerogative of ownership; therefore, the owners felt comfortable setting those parameters. The other three goals would have different measurements depending on the customers being focused on, the group or department doing the work, and the individuals within that group.

Obstacles

Next up was to determine where they were to achieve demonstrable improvement in each of the four areas. The 120 attendees broke into small groups to discuss the obstacles that currently blocked them from the goals. Each group focused on what it perceived to be the three or four main obstacles. The entire group listed all the obstacles and debated which ones were primary, finally determining them to be: (1) lack of an adequate way to measure performance, and (2) bonuses not being directly tied to performance and distributed too infrequently (twice per year for hourly paid workers and once per year for salaried workers) to have a major impact. People volunteered to serve on action teams to address each of these obstacles.

The results of the summit conference were presented at a half-day meeting of the entire company. All in attendance were provided with the opportunity to join one of the action teams. Prior to implementing solutions, the action teams needed to bring their recommendations back to the original large group for agreement. This step was not for approval; rather, it was to ensure that all those doing the work had answered the critical questions prior to implementation. If all questions were answered, there was no need for formal approval—action could begin.

PHASE 4: MOVING FORWARD WITH PERFORMANCE MANAGEMENT AND REWARDS

Performance management and rewards became the main focus in phase 4. The solution to the obstacles mentioned—lack of performance criteria and the inadequacies of the bonus system—ended up being one and the same. The team addressing this issue transformed the Company Performance Share into the "Great Performance Share" (GPS).

Internal Customer Needs and Contract

Under the GPS system, work teams (whether functional or project based) or individuals contact their internal customers on a monthly basis to determine what each customer needs from them to do their own work better. Once agreement is reached, a performance contract is developed.

To keep everyone moving in the same direction, each contract must fall within one of the Four Ideal End States. Developing the contract may take place in direct meetings or it may be done via e-mail. If necessary, negotiation brings individuals to a common understanding.

The contract may be valid for up to six months as long as there is a demonstration of action toward the goal each month. The team then meets to determine what individual members will do to ensure they meet the terms of their contract. At the end of the month, a simple questionnaire is sent to the internal customer(s): Are we meeting and/or making progress toward our contract? If the response is in the affirmative, the process moves to the next step, distribution of the Great Performance Share.

Dividing the Profits

Each Great Performance Share approximates the total monthly profits divided by the total number of people working in the company. If the contract includes an entire team, the team gets the equivalent of one share for each member. The team then splits the GPS among the individual team members.

This system rewards the performance of those providing products or services to others in the company. It also requires individuals throughout the organization to be learning constantly, as the contracts generally provide for performance above and beyond what is required in workers' basic jobs. Workers are always looking for what their customers need. They are, therefore, always thinking and being creative in their work.

Feedback systems provide the information individuals need in order to know if they are doing a good job. All contracts are listed on Johnsonville's computer-based electronic bulletin board. On a weekly basis information is added to the contract to identify what actions were taken to meet the established goal. All employees have access to the bulletin board, and anyone can comment on the performance contract of anyone else.

Reexamining Performance

During this period, a summit conference, later called the "Great Performance Meeting," took place every six months. Most of the 700 members of the company got together twice each year to reexamine where they were going. Individual participants were responsible for going back to the members of their various teams (functional, cross-functional, or task) who did not attend the conference and reporting on the discussion. Each team then discussed how any new developments would affect it and their customers. These conversations were used to determine the next round of GP contracts.

The company had now transitioned to a fluid format. Everyone, including the company ownership, was involved in determining where the company was going. Small groups formed themselves based on the task at hand. They determined what needed to be accomplished, involving those who would be affected by whatever was done. Information systems were put in place to provide everyone with complete information about what was happening and where. The Four Ideal End States established at the initial summit conference served to help all members evaluate their own performance.

SUMMARY

Johnsonville Sausage has conceptual DNA as its foundation. Now-CEO Ralph Stayer's "Leading the Journey Model," which was designed for the creation of personal responsibility—as described in his book *Flight of the Buffalo* (Belasco and Stayer 1993)—provides a guidepost for action by members of the company. This model is used at the summit conference. The ideal is first identified by those who need to work toward it. This same group identifies the obstacles that will keep the organization from moving toward that ideal. As a third step, the individuals or work groups who will be directly affected by any change work together to find a way to remove the obstacles.

Again, the other three DNA types—factual, contextual, and individual—are present in this organization, but they are defined and interpreted by the dominant conceptual DNA in systematically different ways. Johnsonville's factual DNA is evident in its daily performance measurement to help individuals determine how to improve. The Four Ideal End States, developed from the Leading the Journey Model, provide a basis for all work conducted in the company. Contextually, employees work together in "Functional Excellence Teams," which provide direction and interactional support toward high performance. Employees learn to take personal responsibility through an individual-focused member development system.

Contextual DNA:
YSI, Inc.

YSI is a company that designs and manufactures precision instruments for the medical industry. Though ostensibly exhibiting a traditional hierarchy with a chairman and CEO at the top, in no place on the organization chart are there more than two layers below vice president—including frontline employees. All production employees, who represent one-third of the company's 295 employees, are listed by work unit and by name.

At YSI, workers do not dress in formal business attire. Managers often come to work wearing shorts, a T-shirt, and tennis shoes. There are no offices, only cubicles. The production floor is actually several mini-production units called "business centers," each of which posts a team picture. There are no time clocks. Within given, broad parameters, people schedule their own work time.

A SHARED DECISION-MAKING CULTURE

Employees make many decisions that directly affect themselves. For instance, in the early 1970s YSI suffered a business downturn. There was a need for layoffs, as there was not enough work for everyone. Rather than management deciding who would be laid off, employees made the decision. They voted to create a rotating layoff system so that each person would be laid off an equal amount of time. When another economic decline some years later necessitated further cost reductions, the employees determined that they would take up the slack by all taking a 4.6 percent reduction in pay. They returned themselves to the previous pay rate when business picked up.

Other decisions are also made in an egalitarian manner. For instance, all employees—those who would traditionally be paid an hourly wage and those traditionally paid a salary—are paid an hourly rate. Although the company adheres to state and federal wage and hour laws by paying overtime to those who would be classified as eligible for such, conceptually and practically all employees are equal.

SHARING THE PROFITS

The company has an employee stock ownership program (ESOP) as well as a profit-sharing plan that is paid out in cash annually. When the latter was first established, profits were shared based on a percentage of one's wages. This meant that those in leadership positions received more in profit sharing than other workers. On a vote by all company employee-owners, this was changed to a policy whereby everyone receives the same amount.

HISTORICAL PERSPECTIVE

In addition to the company's egalitarian roots, a long-standing tradition has been its family-friendly atmosphere. If employees need time to deal with a family member's health care or would like to attend a child's program at school, they simply schedule it. There is no problem as long as workers put in forty hours weekly. Each person is responsible for recording his or her own hours worked. A falsified time sheet, however, is grounds for termination.

Another component of YSI's historic development is the company's connection to Antioch College, which is located in YSI's hometown of Yellow Springs, Ohio. Antioch is an experimental college that encourages students to explore new ideas. The company's three founders are Antioch graduates; they began their business in the basement of the college. Interestingly, Douglas McGregor was a member of the Antioch faculty until the 1960s. His well-known philosophy of social equity and industrial democracy and his "Theory Y" style of management, which posits that managers can have more success leading in a humanitarian manner than autocratically (McGregor 1960), provide a theoretical base for much of the work approach found at YSI. For example, evolving from McGregor's teaching, the company has experimented with different types of teams over the years.

A DIFFERENT KIND OF TEAM STRUCTURE

The modified hierarchy is just one of several structures in place. The work process has evolved into an interconnected system of teams including both functional and cross-functional teams. Some of these structures serve multiple purposes, such as getting work done and sharing information.

Functional Teams

The fixed, permanent teams are each responsible for a specific functional job. Other teams are more short-lived: they are formed to address specific issues and usually reach their goals and dissolve after a meeting or two.

At the very core of the company are the production workers, who are organized into business centers. These are the functional work groups that produce the monitoring devices the company sells. There are ten business centers ranging in size from three to twenty-three workers.

Some business centers operate as self-directed teams. They receive a schedule of work to be completed every other morning that lists the quantity of each product to be made and the date it is due to the customer. Orders with imminent due dates receive the highest priority. Workers have learned how to read their own production schedule and take care of their own materials. Throughout the day, when one person finishes a job he or she goes to the production schedule and takes the order that has the next-highest priority. This degree of autonomy is feasible partly because each customer's job order is accompanied by a list of components and the process for building the product.

While some business centers just follow the procedures they are given, others have been proactive in updating these standards. For example, when assembly procedure manuals are inaccurate or too technically worded for new employees, the team might rewrite and submit them to the process engineer on their own volition.

While the production schedule is based on customer demand, business center members create their own work schedule. The company has broad guidelines stating that work must be done between 6:00 a.m. and 6:00 p.m. and that each person is expected to work forty hours per week. Members simply work within these parameters.

To coordinate activities and communications, each business center has a "point person" who serves as the team communicator. Point persons attend weekly role meetings to keep up on issues related to the company and production scheduling. A different person serves as point person each month, and all business center members serve in the position at one time or another.

Resource people, such as the process engineer and planner, support the business centers. The business centers also have access to a safety coordinator, a purchasing agent, a scheduler, and a quality-control person. One production coordinator works with all business centers in personal development as well as in facilitating interpersonal and informational issues.

To keep members informed on production issues and performance, each business center holds at least one monthly meeting. Members and their support staffs use these meetings to check on service being provided, to share information, and to review the business center's performance.

Cross-Functional Teams

In addition to functional teams, there are a number of ways YSI employee-owners collaborate cross-functionally. Cross-functional teams exist in several different forms; some are specifically focused on a product line. Membership consists of anyone who has an impact on that specific product including Customer Service, Purchasing, Engineering, and Production. The business center member who attends is the point person for that month. This approach facilitates a greater understanding of the specific customer's needs and underscores that the entire organization is one big team.

When a new product is to be designed, a development team is created to take the product through concept development and an exploration of market viability, including the development of a prototype, development of expense and capital budgets, cost-benefit analysis, and test marketing. This cross-functional team includes members who have impact on the product—they will be involved in producing it, selling it, and dealing with the customer after its purchase.

Each cross-functional team has a team leader who provides coordination and keeps its meetings focused. Once established, these teams tend to be very interactive, with every member participating. When a new product is at its final stages, the development team does not make the final "go or no go" decision; it makes a recommendation to the management team. Provided that there is a payback on the product and that it meets other criteria for success, the management team will generally approve the team's recommendation.

Some cross-functional teams have a charge that is not directly work related, such as the responsibility for the YSI Foundation, which is administered by four employee-owners located throughout the company. The foundation provides support for cultural, educational, environmental, scientific, and social community projects. In 1997 the YSI Foundation disbursed grants in excess of $100,000 to over twenty-five of these projects.

Not all teams are formally organized. You can walk through the facility and see people gathering spontaneously to deal with one issue or another. Generally an employee recognizes an issue or an opportunity and then talks with others who may be affected. They meet once, or more, if necessary; the issue gets addressed, and then the team is dissolved.

Other Collaborations

There are other forms of collaboration that are not so easily identified. The Leadership Council, for example, is a group of approximately thirty members who are selected by the CEO. Their role in their twice-monthly meeting is that of a sounding board, although they also have significant input on company direction. For instance, a strategic initiative to focus on ecological sustainability came from this team. To identify this goal, four subteams of the Leadership Council were formed with leaders appointed by the CEO. Each team was charged with discussing a series of questions to determine a strategy on which the company could agree.

COMMUNICATION

A company-wide meeting is held at least once each quarter, led by the company president, although others may have roles to play. The meetings provide an opportunity for members to share information about the performance of the company, such as its current financial situation, new products that are being developed, the standing of the company in the marketplace, and other issues of concern. Company-wide meetings may be called for special events, such as the unveiling of a new company sign in front of the facility, or sometimes just for a general celebration.

An unusual communications forum is the CEO's monthly birthday lunches. All those who have a birthday in any given month are invited to a group luncheon with the CEO. During the luncheon, each person in attendance is given the opportunity to ask the president any question of interest or to voice a concern. It's also an opportunity for the CEO to share ideas informally and to receive feedback on those ideas.

Performance Agreement and Development Plan

Each member of the organization creates a performance agreement and a development plan that covers accountability, short-term goals, long-term goals, and learning units. It is a living document that is officially revisited twice a year. In addition to identifying what they agree to regarding performance, individual employee-owners select several other company members who see their work on a regular basis to assess them.

The performance agreement is then used as the basis for a conversation about development. A specific development plan, with related coursework, is written up and signed by the employee-owner and his or her leader. In the case of production workers, the production coordinator facilitates each individual's performance agreement.

The Council on Education and Development (COED) was formed to acknowledge the importance of continuing education for all company employee-owners. The COED requires that each individual take two "learning units" each year. While there is no strict definition of what a learning unit is, generally it is a class.

Hiring

The team process is reinforced by a system of hiring new employees to fit the culture, orienting them to that culture, assisting them in measuring their own performance, and rewarding them for the work they do. The hiring process is designed to provide a high level of probability that a new employee will fit into the company. In the production area employees may begin in part-time or temporary positions.

Often, in hiring from outside the company, direct experience or even appropriate skills for the job appear to be irrelevant. For instance, the production supervisor we talked to had no previous supervisory experience. An engineer was asked a series of questions about previous experience. She was surprised when she was hired for the job since she answered "no" to all of them. What appears to be more important is the ability to fit into the culture and the willingness to learn the job.

Orientation

The work practices at YSI are different from those at most other companies. Most YSI employees don't begin work with the knowledge of how to work in such a system. The New Employee Orientation Network (NEON) program attempts to help employees understand how to work at YSI. In the first tier of the program employees receive orientation over a two-week period from an assigned buddy. As another sign of the company's egalitarian atmosphere, new leaders can "buddy up" with production workers and vice versa. New employees spend some time going to each of the organization's major functional areas, meeting those who do the work, being introduced to the product and how it works, and learning about the customer base. A flyer introducing the new employee is sent to all employee-owners. An orientation schedule lists where the new employee will be, along with information about that person. In the program's annual second tier, that year's hires have lunch with the members of the management team and respond to a series of questions about the company and what it was like to be a new employee.

Performance Measurement

Once employees become comfortable with the organization, a number of mechanisms are in place to help them know how well they are doing. While receiving feedback from co-workers happens formally only twice a year, other systems are in place to help workers determine performance on a daily basis. Production statistics such as on-time delivery and quality data are reported at team meetings. Individuals have ways to keep track of their performance based on what is expected of them and reinforced through the reward systems.

Reward Systems

YSI has several reward systems, some compensation related. One process allows an employee-owner to nominate any individual or team for special recognition for performance "above and beyond the call of duty." A team evaluates these nominations, and those selected receive a small cash stipend.

The all-hourly workforce has a "broadband" approach to pay: two job designations and pay ranges cover all business center members. In addition, the company has an ESOP that allows all employees to own a bit of the company. This "sense of ownership" has led to greater commitment to the company's success and is an important component of the overall YSI philosophy. Two employee-owners have a seat on the board of directors.

Interpersonal Conflicts

While most interpersonal issues are usually dealt with immediately, at times this is not the case. The company offers conflict resolution classes, but the relevant skills are not always implemented. It seems that some individuals would rather ignore the problems than confront them. If conflict is interfering with performance or if assistance is requested, the production coordinator will step in to assist the individuals in resolving the conflict.

SUMMARY

Contextual DNA–based YSI is a relatively open organization with no hard list of rules to follow and no handbook to tell workers exactly what to do. Even the exact formula for an ideal organization is not established. What is commonly understood, though, is that teams will provide the basis for the organizational structure. As this organization has evolved, a level of egalitarianism—the Antioch College influence—and the team atmosphere have remained. At times there are disagreements over specifics, but the one thing members do agree on is the kind of company they can all be proud of: one that is family friendly, part of the community they come from, and complementary with the environment in which they live.

Once again, the other three DNA types—factual, conceptual, and individual—are present in this organization, but they are defined and interpreted by the dominant contextual DNA in systematically different ways.

Factual information at YSI is made known through widespread information sharing, often in face-to-face meetings. YSI's overriding concept is the philosophy of social equity and industrial democracy as encouraged by Douglas McGregor. Individuals see their values reflected through the mission of the organization.

Individual DNA:
Wainwright Industries

Wainwright Industries manufactures critical-tolerance machined and stamped aircraft parts as well as electric motor housings for automobile power wipers and power windows. It has received several prestigious awards including the Malcolm Baldrige Quality Award in the small business category, and it was selected in 1996 by *Industry Week* as one of the ten best manufacturing facilities in the United States.

This family-owned firm involves employees in most aspects of the business process, from setting strategic direction to the purchase and layout of new machinery to day-to-day issues such as how work will be accomplished. The whole process revolves around a concept they've used as the title for a video, *Sincere Trust and Belief in People* (Wainwright 1997). At Wainwright it is the individual who is most valued.

HISTORICAL PERSPECTIVE

While trying to determine why a Total Quality Management (TQM) process implemented in the company was not as successful as hoped, management realized that they did not trust employees to make their own decisions. In examining the basis for this belief, they determined that the workers did not have the knowledge and information they needed to make decisions. This became the starting point for a new approach to TQM and to leading the organization.

All employees, whom they refer to as "associates," were provided with the opportunity to have their personal skills assessed off-site at a local technical college. Recommendations were then made for individual development. All personal development activities were also conducted off-site and, unless they notified their colleagues, no one knew what others were working on. The company then provided "soft" skills training to everyone. Topics included problem solving and giving and accepting constructive feedback. Learning and development became keys to organizational success.

MISSION

A small group composed mostly of managers was selected to create the first draft of a mission statement. The draft was distributed to everybody in the company for their comments. One of the recipients, a janitor, summarized the message by noting the company's "continuous commitment to our customers' future." It was a simple and easily understandable observation, and it was adopted. This caused the leadership to question its original decision not to include the rank and file in the early discussions. They began to realize that they had not trusted employees to do the right thing without guidance from management.

As a result, when identifying the strategic issues for attention, and given the mission statement, management began asking all employees what they believed was most important in their doing a good job. They received hundreds of comments and found that these fell into five main categories (which were finally adopted as the company's goals):

◊ Safety

◊ Employee involvement/satisfaction

◊ Customer satisfaction

◊ Product quality

◊ Financial performance

The first two are performance indicators; they deal with the people in the organization. The latter three are results indicators that deal with organizational performance and are considered direct consequences of the performance indicators.

At the center of the organization, literally and figuratively, is the "Mission Control" room. This room, used for meetings on a regular basis, makes visible the key strategies the company follows to fulfill its mission. On the walls are plaques displaying the company's five strategic goals. There is a plaque for each company customer as well. A green flag above an individual customer or client plaque indicates that performance is at or above goal. A red flag is cause for immediate action because it indicates that performance has dropped below goal. Posted beneath each plaque are charts tracking performance along with the name of the manager primarily responsible.

PERFORMANCE INDICATORS

Of the two primary performance indicators, safety has the highest priority and is watched more closely than any of the other indicators. This is in line with the belief that employees have to be safe in order to do their job. Every accident or near-accident in the facility is reenacted and videotaped. With the assistance of a trainer, the person involved

in the incident narrates the reenactment. The video is shown to everyone in the company during departmental meetings. Recordable acci-
dents, days since the last lost-time accident, and the number of
employee safety suggestions each week are tracked on charts in each
department. A consolidated version is posted in Mission Control. The
ever-present green and red flags indicate to anyone passing by the
room whether or not they are meeting company goals.

The second most important performance indicator is employee
involvement/satisfaction. Employee satisfaction is measured by an
internal customer satisfaction index (ICSI). On a quarterly basis, associates are afforded the opportunity to grade the performance of their
managers, such as the quality department manager, which they rely
on to get their job done. Each manager's grades are translated into
number scores, aggregated, and posted in Mission Control. The com-
posite ICSI is measured against the company goal for the area. A failure to meet the goals is indicated by a red flag over the chart and is
cause for immediate action.

Employee involvement is measured through the Continuous Improvement Program (CIP). Employees are responsible for developing
CIP ideas as well as implementing them. These could include actions
such as placing a hazard cone next to a raised track to prevent workers
from tripping on it, labeling the capacity of storage shelves to avoid
overloading, and adding a bar to prevent boxes from slipping into an
aisle. The company is not necessarily looking for high-impact changes
through the ideas implemented; small dollar savings add up.

Only implemented ideas are rewarded. If a worker has an idea, he or
she implements it personally or gets assistance from co-workers. After
implementation, the idea is written up and submitted to a supervisor.
The supervisor signs off on it as an "information-only" step. Each CIP
idea is recorded on a chart posted in each department. The departmental CIP idea totals are transferred to a master chart in Mission
Control.

Wainwright considers safety and the Continuous Improvement Program so important that these are specifically rewarded. Names of the employees who submit improvements are entered into a weekly drawing for a cash award, but if the implemented item is related to a safety concern, it is entered into a separate drawing to emphasize the importance of this issue. The dollar value of the improvement is not considered.

RESULTS INDICATORS

Customer satisfaction is on the list of company performance metrics and is measured by an external customer satisfaction index (CSI). Each month any customer who represents more than .5 percent of the company's business, and who has agreed to do so, receives a survey asking them to rate the company's performance on communication, quality, performance, and delivery. Each customer's grades are posted in the department responsible for making the product and under each customer's chart in Mission Control. A grade of B or lower requires a corrective action plan—to be developed, posted, and communicated to the customer within forty-eight hours.

A "customer champion" selected at the beginning of each fiscal year and the customer service representative or quality manager head up all internal action related to that customer. The customer champion, who may be a production worker, is selected by the customer service manager in conjunction with the production manager. Champions attend a short training class presented by the customer service and quality managers to learn what is expected of them and about processes for finding root causes of problems.

At Wainwright, product quality is as important to the company as customer satisfaction. Yet, there are no quality inspectors; rather, each production employee is responsible for his or her own work quality based on systems that are put in place by the quality manager in conjunction with each work area.

ISO 9002 and QS 9000, internationally recognized processes created to certify the quality of manufacturing and quality processes, are the tools for maintaining disciplined documentation. As with each of the other measures, performance in terms of meeting product quality goals is posted in each department and in Mission Control.

Reflecting the CEO's vision of running the company with a combination of democratic participation, Christian values, and a bit of Zen philosophy (Wainwright 1997), financial performance is the last item on the list of results indicators. The belief is that if the other four criteria are taken care of, the financial results will come.

ASSOCIATE PERFORMANCE DEVELOPMENT PLAN

All employees have a performance development plan in place. Twice each year supervisors meet individually with each of them in Mission Control to review what the employee has done well in the past six months and to choose two areas that he or she can further develop over the next six months to support the overall company goals. Performance deficiencies are handled on an ongoing basis, not at these planning meetings. Employees can work continually on their interpersonal and job-specific skills to help them achieve those goals. Toward that end, the company spends approximately 7 percent of its payroll on development and training.

To further enhance the focus on development, most positions are filled from within the company. The underlying directive is to allow everyone to use his or her talents to be the best they can be. Over 60 percent of the employees in the company have been promoted at least once; some have been promoted several times.

SUPPORT SYSTEMS

The company's focus on performance did not happen automatically. A good deal of work went into creating systems that support it. With the philosophy that "what is best for people must be defined in their terms," management has made a basic shift in relationships among people at work.

Now there is an egalitarian atmosphere. Symbolically, all members of the company, including the CEO, wear an identical uniform with their first name over the left breast pocket and a "Team Wainwright" patch over the right. A profit-sharing system is in place to divide a portion of the profits equally among all employees.

All company meetings are held in Mission Control. Since this is where the company's strategic goals and performance data are tracked, this keeps the data in everyone's view on a regular basis. The red and green flags make performance very visible. Also found in Mission Control is a symbol and reminder of how things used to be: a stool the CEO once threw across a room when frustrated with company performance and his inability to make necessary changes on his own.

Language is used carefully. Employees are "associates." The human resources department has been renamed "The People Zone." Problems are expressed as "opportunities." Mistakes are seen as "opportunities for improvement"; managers and supervisors make a conscious effort not to punish employees for their errors.

Teamwork is an overriding theme. While teams are not used as an organizing structure, there are constant references to the company as Team Wainwright. People do work together on an ongoing basis, and, as indicated earlier, project teams are developed to address customer concerns as the need arises.

Functional groups work together on a daily basis and meet regularly to discuss the performance of their units and of the company. Cross-functional teams are used on one-time or intractable issues. They focus on specific projects such as reorganizing the office or reengineering the way housings are made or how piston struts are machined. These teams tend to form around a specific issue and disband when the projects are completed.

The most prevalent teams are those that might be labeled "spontaneous teams." These ad hoc teams are generally formed when there is a customer service or quality issue. A problem is identified, and the customer champion forms a team that can address the opportunity. The team dissolves as soon as the issue is resolved.

COMPENSATION SYSTEMS

There are two compensation systems at Wainwright. The wage system is based on the individual job. Upon hire, employees are introduced to a training matrix listing what they need to know at each job level. Upon completion of training at each level, they must pass a certification. Each level has a pay range associated with it, divided into six-month segments. Except in extreme circumstances, employees reach the top of their pay range within two years. They then receive only minimal cost-of-living pay increases until they move into a new job level.

The second system is the profit-sharing program. Up to 25 percent of company profits are split equally among all workers and managers twice each year. The money is placed into a 401(k) plan that is administered by an employee-run team.

ORGANIZATIONAL STRUCTURE

The company is structured in a hierarchical arrangement with defined roles. The strategic planning group, composed of the three co-owners of the company, works on long-term strategy—three to five years into the future—not on day-to-day operations. It meets weekly for a status check on how the company is performing to the set strategic indicators. All plans and decisions are related to the company's operating values, including five strategic directives: customer-driven quality, continuous improvement, fast response, design for quality and defect prevention, and full participation.

The Operations Group is responsible for day-to-day leadership and consists of the operations leader, department managers, and administrative managers from departments including Accounting and Human Resources. They also meet weekly.

The analogy of "positions on the bus" has been used to describe the roles throughout the company. Leadership is sitting in the back of the bus to make sure it is on the right road and going in the right direction. Middle management, empowered to run the business, drives the bus, and the workforce sits in the seats behind middle management, telling them which way to turn and how far to go. All are involved in doing and improving work.

BELIEF IN ITS PEOPLE

Company employees attest that the company's belief in its people is reflected throughout the organization. Wainwright Industries has long had a "no layoff unless absolutely necessary" policy. In 1998 a labor strike at a customer's company challenged this approach. Rather than lay people off, the company had employees do preventive maintenance and attend training programs throughout the strike. They told them, however, that at some point the cash would run out and a layoff would be necessary. When the strike went beyond the limit of what the company could afford, people were in fact laid off. The owners announced they would fund the extension of the workers' unemployment compensation up to a defined date. The strike ended approximately one week prior to the expiration of the additional financial support.

The company's "no secrets" policy means that information is shared widely. With the exception of salaries, virtually all data are available to anyone in the company. The profit-and-loss statement is shared with all employees on a monthly basis.

SUMMARY

Wainwright Industries' individual DNA determines the value it puts on the individual employee. The company's focus on the individual is expressed in statements made by managers such as "we beat the path while walking," implying that rather than having preset rules and regulations, issues will be addressed as they arise (Honold 1999).

The other three DNA types—factual, conceptual, and contextual—are present in this organization, but they are defined and interpreted by the dominant individual DNA in systematically different ways. Factual information at Wainwright is made known through its safety and employee involvement/satisfaction programs. The underlying conceptual basis is Total Quality Management, which is focused on individual performance. The context is best reflected by Mission Control, which connects the office area to the plant and provides a visual format for the company goals. The emphasis on the individual is reflected by the company's video *Sincere Trust and Belief in People* describing the management process at Wainwright.

Embedded DNA Types

The organizations detailed in the previous chapters are described to demonstrate the four types of organizations by DNA type, but they also reflect the complexity of this model. Each of the organizations has a dominant DNA type, and each DNA is reflected within it. So, for instance, the factual DNA–based organization, Springfield Remanufacturing Corporation, also manifests its conceptual, contextual, and individual DNA under the dominant rubric (see table 1, page 45). How these dimensions factor into the company's operations depends on the dominant DNA.

It is critical for a company that its dominant type and its associated dimensions be in alignment. In our judgment, misalignment is the major cause of organizational ineffectiveness and individual performance failures.

As we will see, alignment between the dominant DNA type and a variety of critical leadership and management practices, such as decision making, development, compensation, and so on, is also important. We will address these topics first through the exemplars of organizations whose practices reflect significant differences in relation to the four types and then extend our treatment in a less descriptive, more prescriptive, manner.

AT SPRINGFIELD REMANUFACTURING CORPORATION (SRC)

As described, SRC's factual DNA is exemplified by its focus on the bottom line, the profit-and-loss statement, including its use of critical numbers charted to ensure that performance is on track for every sub-unit facility. The other types of DNA are expressed in a manner consistent with the dominant type, as we see below.

The central concept driving company operations is the capitalist enterprise. Capitalism is stressed in employee education, in outreach to the community—including a program showing third graders how to establish a mini-business—and in spin-off companies that exploit opportunities to generate additional revenue.

The context created for developing employee interaction is the weekly staff meeting. Week in and week out the same groups meet to focus on the balance sheet and review performance. Even the interpersonal relationships are integrated into the organization through these meetings. At the corporate staff meeting a major portion of the agenda is reserved for personal announcements.

The main component that ties the individual to the company is the employee stock ownership program (ESOP). Each employee who has

Table 1   Dominant and Subsidiary DNA Types and Exemplifications

---

Springfield Remanufacturing Corporation

Factual DNA	Profit-and-loss statement
Conceptual DNA	Capitalism
Contextual DNA	Staff meetings
Individual DNA	ESOP

Johnsonville Sausage

Conceptual DNA	Leading the Journey Model and Four Ideal End States
Factual DNA	Daily performance measurement
Contextual DNA	Functional Excellence Teams
Individual DNA	Member development; personal responsibility

YSI, Inc.

Contextual DNA	Interdependent teams
Factual DNA	Face-to-face information sharing
Conceptual DNA	Social equity and industrial democracy
Individual DNA	Values embedded in mission

Wainwright Industries

Individual DNA	*Sincere Trust and Belief in People* video
Factual DNA	Safety and employee involvement/satisfaction
Conceptual DNA	Total Quality Management
Contextual DNA	Mission Control

---

been employed for at least one year owns some small portion of the company. This measured sense of belonging increases with each subsequent year of employment.

AT JOHNSONVILLE SAUSAGE

At conceptual DNA–based Johnsonville Sausage, operations are guided by a vision, namely the Leading the Journey Model as described in Ralph Stayer's book *Flight of the Buffalo*. This model, coupled with the Four Ideal End States (see page 17) leads all members of the organization to the guiding principle of personal responsibility. The other types of DNA at Johnsonville are influenced by the concept that each person is responsible for his or her own performance.

Daily performance measurements serve as the key factual determinants for improvement. The Great Performance Share, which is based on a specific contract, provides additional measurement, but it too is based on making employees responsible for their own performance.

The work context is largely a system of teams. These teams are based not so much on relationships as they are on individuals needing to work with others to get their job done. Functional Excellence Teams keep everyone working together toward the same goals and keep the central concept of personal responsibility at the forefront.

Individual employees also have the opportunity to continually improve themselves through a member development system. This system is available to all but, in the spirit of personal responsibility, is not mandatory.

AT YSI, INC.

The essence of YSI is exemplified by its contextual DNA as demonstrated by the interdependencies of its team-based culture. Teams are responsible for producing products, developing new products, determining how to invest the company's community contributions, and determining how best to implement a philosophy of ecological sustainability.

Factual material is made known through widespread information sharing, often in face-to-face meetings, as opposed to formal written reports.

The driving concepts are social equity and industrial democracy as developed by Douglas McGregor (1960) in his Theory Y style of management while president of Antioch College and later as a Harvard professor—advanced through the context of the interdependent teams.

Individuals see their personal values reflected in the mission of the organization, accomplished through the actions of the interdependent teams.

AT WAINWRIGHT INDUSTRIES

Wainwright Industries exhibits its individual DNA—and a strong commitment to the individual stakeholder of the company—through its published video titled *Sincere Trust and Belief in People*. Management at Wainwright trusts that people want to be involved in improving their workplace. Building on that trust, managers train employees to take on more responsibility.

Factual performance goals are tracked, but they are highlighted in terms of individual performance enhancing employee safety or the contributions of individual employees.

The underlying philosophic concept driving the company is Total Quality Management. The owner and several managers from the company spent significant time in Japan learning how to use TQM to integrate individuals into the organization.

Mission Control provides the context for individual assessment and the visual reinforcement of beliefs.

SUMMARY

The existence of a dominant DNA type does not suggest that the embedded types are unimportant. Rather, each aligns with the dominant type. Problems occur when there is misalignment between them. The variations associated with leadership and management practices and opportunities for alignment and misalignment are the focus of part 2.

PART

Two

Aligning Practices
with DNA

E ach DNA type suggests organizational practices that are specific to that type. In part 2 we provide ways for you to identify areas of practice and DNA misalignment in your company. Aligning your practices will relieve organizational stress.

We begin by examining leadership practices such as mission development, governance structure, and executive/managerial leadership. Next, we look at management practices such as planning, teamwork, and performance management. We then observe human resources practices and how employees are hired, promoted, compensated, and developed. Finally, we examine everyday cultural practices and issues such as decision making, how interpersonal relationships develop, how change occurs, and how profits are viewed. Our larger goal is to recognize that alignment is required between an organization's DNA and the way in which its practices and operations are understood and executed.

At the time our four exemplar organizations were studied, each reflected its particular DNA in the ways it accomplished its work. Given the dynamic nature of organizations, the practices described may have changed. Reflected here is what was present at a specific point in time. The practices serve as models from which we extrapolate lessons for organizational improvement through the use of the organizational DNA model. These examples will suggest the alignment of the practices with the basic character of the organizations as known through their dominant DNA types.

Leadership Practices

L eadership practices fashion organizations. They provide the foundations for strategic and tactical directions, tacit and explicit communication, stakeholder satisfaction, and social influence.

Traditionally, leaders are charged with pronouncing and developing their vision for the organization in a way that directs action. They are also responsible for allowing others to become engaged as they adopt the motivating perspective that gives life to their work setting.

Our four organizations reflect leadership practices that are congruent with their DNA types. Aspects of leadership that will be examined here include the development of the mission, the governance structure, and the act of leading itself.

MISSION PURPOSE

The existence of a mission statement serves as a focusing element for employees of an organization. As illustrated in table 2, we found a different mission purpose and manifestation in each of the four DNA types.

Table 2 Mission Purpose and DNA Alignment

DNA Type	Company	Mission Purpose	Manifestation
Factual	Springfield (SRC)	Specify the goal	15% per year growth; no formal mission statement
Conceptual	Johnsonville	Set the vision	Four Ideal End States based on individual responsibility
Contextual	YSI	Provide for linked foundations	McGregor's Theory Y; quality; ecological sustainability
Individual	Wainwright	Identify indicators of success	Key strategic indicators: safety, employee involvement/satisfaction, customer satisfaction, product quality, and financial results

Factual DNA: Factual DNA–based Springfield Remanufacturing Corporation (SRC) does not have a formal mission statement. Yet, as you talk to employees about the company's mission in terms of goals, you find that every employee is acutely aware of it. The company's goals are to grow at a rate of 15 percent per year and to maintain a high-quality product. Both goals are objectified through the profit-and-loss statement as reported in the weekly meetings.

Conceptual DNA: Conceptual DNA–based Johnsonville Sausage has a mission statement that declares a moral responsibility to become the best sausage company in the world and states that each employee must take responsibility for his or her own performance to ensure that this occurs. Based on the mission and providing the basis for all work done in the company are its Four Ideal End States: (1) make the best products; (2) provide outstanding service; (3) have industry-leading financial results; and (4) provide the best workplace. Each of these requires "superlative performance" by each individual employee.

Contextual DNA: Contextual DNA–based YSI has several components to its mission: to practice McGregor's humanistic Theory Y approach to management, to maintain high quality, and to provide for ecological sustainability.

Douglas McGregor served as an inspiration for the founders of the company, who were all graduates of Antioch College, where McGregor served as president. As they endeavored to carry out his humanistic philosophy, the company evolved into a team-based organization wherein the group determines who will work on what and all share responsibility for leading the team. As YSI manufactures medical instruments, quality is an absolute requirement. Yet, work teams assist technical personnel in determining how the quality products will be manufactured.

The company's emphasis on ecological sustainability was derived from an employee focus group asked to uncover what was important to those who work at YSI. All components of the mission are derived from the relationships that developed in the context of teams and personal relationships.

Individual DNA: Individual DNA–based Wainwright Industries provides a constant visual reminder of employees' performance against the company's five key strategic indicators in its centralized Mission Control room. These indicators provide the framework for all activity at the company. The first two performance indicators are the most critical, as both are related to the well-being of the individual: safety and employee involvement/satisfaction.

Each individual is responsible for his or her own safety. When an accident or near-accident occurs, it is reenacted by the person involved and is videotaped and shared with others in the area.

As a measure of employee satisfaction, those who report to managers also grade them on their performance. A grade below an A triggers a one-on-one conversation between the employee and the manager to get to the bottom of the difficulty and to work out differences. The Continuous Improvement Program (CIP) measures employee involvement. Employees are encouraged not only to come up with ideas for improvement to work procedures, but also to implement them on their own, even if it means incurring a cost. The number of CIP ideas implemented is used as an evaluation tool in determining performance toward this goal.

The results indicators include customer satisfaction, product quality, and financial performance. Customer satisfaction is rated through a grading process conducted quarterly. Product quality is measured with traditional metrics such as a count of rejected parts and warranty returns.

The owners of the company firmly believe that if safety, internal and external customer satisfaction, and product quality are taken care of adequately, positive financial results will follow. Therefore, the financial numbers are merely tracked, not actively worked toward.

As we've seen, each organization's mission—whether explicit or implicit—reflects its dominant DNA type. Just as important, each dominant DNA type effectively incorporates the other, subsidiary, types; that is, the subsidiary types of DNA are embedded in the dominant type. Thus, Johnsonville sees its individual employees as champions of its vision, while Wainwright measures and develops factual performance data using individuals as its primary orientation. The individual has a significantly different meaning in these two settings determined by their different DNA.

GOVERNANCE STRUCTURE

Most organizations have adopted a hierarchical structure. Each of our four empowering organizations has a leadership and/or leadership

Table 3   Governance Structure and DNA Alignment

DNA Type	Company	Governance Structure	Manifestation
Factual	Springfield (SRC)	Hierarchical	Weekly meeting structure; ESOP
Conceptual	Johnsonville	Concentric	Personal responsibility; family owned
Contextual	YSI	Federated (multiple centers of leadership)	Egalitarian; team focus; ESOP
Individual	Wainwright	Federated democracy; loosely woven	Family owned; clearly defined group roles

group, but, as you can see in table 3, they take forms that project each company's dominant DNA.

Factual DNA: As might be expected, SRC has a traditional hierarchical structure. The leadership sees to it that goals are set and adhered to. Clear lines of responsibility and accountability are provided within the framework of a system of weekly meetings that begins at the local, plant floor, level and progresses to the entire plant and then the entire company. Operational roles are clearly defined. While the company maintains an employee stock ownership program (ESOP), with 35 percent of company stock held in an employee-owned trust, it is clearly management that determines the overall operational framework.

Conceptual DNA: The governance structure of family-owned Johnsonville Sausage is concentric, with the leadership team—composed of owners and other managers—in the center. The leadership team provides direction and puts in place systems that transfer responsibility to other teams, such as Functional Excellence Teams, and individuals. For instance, the work team budget reinforces employees' taking responsibility for achieving financial results, and the compensation system rewards them for taking responsibility. Each person in the company is like a manager, as each has responsibility for his or her own performance. Should they not perform up to standard, members of their work team will address the issue with them.

Contextual DNA: YSI is an ESOP company with two employee members, selected by co-workers, serving on its board of directors. YSI's management team leads strategy and oversees the company's team-based structure. Issues of day-to-day governance, such as who will work when and with whom, are addressed at the team level.

Key issues in the organization's direction are also resolved in teams. A team led by the CEO, for instance, created the mission. Using a group process, the mission emerged from discussions of what was important to both the organization and the individuals within it.

Individual DNA: Family-owned Wainwright Industries is governed by the owners, who create overall strategy with an eye to the big picture. It is the managers who provide the ongoing, day-to-day leadership. The employees determine how best to do what the leaders have determined needs to be done. While there are various levels, individual roles are clear even though they sometimes overlap.

Each organization's dominant DNA determines how the structure is formed and the roles within it. The factual DNA–based organization clearly delineates who is responsible for what. The conceptual DNA–based organization has leadership that, in addition to providing strategic direction, sees it as their role to incorporate the CEO's philosophy into operations. The structure of the contextual DNA–based organization is made up of interdependent teams. The individual DNA–based organization has well-defined roles for employees and a strong emphasis on personal responsibility.

LEADERSHIP STYLE

Actual hands-on leadership style is also determined by each organization's DNA type. Table 4 depicts the different styles exemplified by the various types.

Table 4 Leadership Style and DNA Alignment

DNA Type	Company	Leadership Style	Manifestation
Factual	Springfield (SRC)	Transactional; responsible for regulating the work of the organization	Setting up system; determining measurements; refraining from day-to-day decision making
Conceptual	Johnsonville	Transformational; reframing issues to address organizational idea	Determining big picture; coaching employees to take responsibility
Contextual	YSI	Adaptive	Setting strategic direction; creating and facilitating work teams
Individual	Wainwright	Interactive	All involved: owners oversee big picture; managers lead on an ongoing basis; employees make improvements as they see fit

Factual DNA: The system of frequent, regularly scheduled meetings and the modified profit-and-loss statements tracking performance were developed by Springfield Remanufacturing's top management. Once these systems were set up and the employees understood and used them, management's job was to make sure that they were followed, allowing leaders to then focus on longer-term strategic issues. Employees are expected to take responsibility and perform their assigned functions.

Conceptual DNA: At Johnsonville Sausage, leadership assists in framing issues of concern and ensures that those affected by an issue are the ones responsible for addressing it. For issues that arise in the course of everyday work, the leadership team serves as a clearing-house, where it cascades issues to relevant plants or functions. If more than one function is affected, a cross-functional team will be formed by those involved. Leadership's role is only to ensure that no affected area that has been left out.

If an issue has company-wide impact, it is addressed at an annual Great Performance Meeting, which is led by employees and involves all employees including those in leadership roles. Task teams are formed to address the issues of concern. These teams dissolve when the issue they are addressing is resolved. The membership of the task team includes anyone who is directly affected by the issue and who wants to be involved. If employees lack knowledge about particular aspects of an issue, it is leadership's role to point them in the direction of proper resources.

Contextual DNA: At YSI the management team is responsible for setting the strategic direction and for creating the company's team-based system. The operations team, just below top management, has created a set of interlocking teams called business centers. Leaders are responsible for coaching and developing people as well as acting as facilitators to bring the right people together to resolve a problem. Most communications are face-to-face, further enhancing teamwork. When new projects or products are identified, the leadership team empowers a cross-functional group to develop the product or project, reserving the final decision-making authority for itself.

Individual DNA: At Wainwright Industries, each stakeholder group has a specific role to play, but roles are generally well-enough defined that individuals have the leeway to make the position their own. So, for instance, leadership set the five strategic indicators used to measure progress but with input from those who work throughout the company. Leadership trusts employees to do the right thing and gives them a high degree of autonomy in addressing issues.

Table 5   Leadership Practices and DNA Alignment

DNA Type	Leadership Practice		
	Mission Purpose	Governance Structure	Leadership Style
Factual	Specify the goal	Hierarchical	Transactional; responsible for regulating the work of the organization
Conceptual	Set the vision	Concentric	Transformational; reframing issues to address organizational idea
Contextual	Provide for linked foundations	Federated (multiple centers of leadership)	Adaptive
Individual	Identify indicators of success	Federated democracy; loosely woven	Interactive

Table 5 summarizes the three leadership practices identified—mission purpose, governance structure, and leadership style—and their alignment with each organization's DNA type. Considering your entire organization, which description do you believe best exemplifies its leadership? Does your answer remain the same when you consider only your working department? Is this the same DNA type that you intuitively selected earlier as you read the type descriptions and the case examples provided? If not, does the misalignment lead to stress or difficulties in your organization?

Management Practices

As with the leadership practices addressed in the previous chapter, approaches to various management practices also vary depending on the organization's DNA. Here we examine planning, teamwork, and performance management. Our four empowering organizations provide very different approaches to these practices.

PLANNING

Organizations have many planning models to choose from. Table 6 illustrates some of them and the specific DNA types with which they align.

Factual DNA: At SRC planning follows the same routine each year. It begins with projections for sales in various areas. Top management then puts together a fairly set corporate plan including the year's critical numbers, which are based on areas of performance shortfall during the previous year. The plan is next delivered to the plants. Each plant has its departments review the plan and make changes based on ability to meet the goals set. This is transmitted back to top management, who may or may not challenge the

Table 6   Planning Process and DNA Alignment

DNA Type	Company	Planning Process	Manifestation
Factual	Springfield (SRC)	Mechanical, routine	Use same model each year
Conceptual	Johnsonville	"Fluid drive": concepts cascade down; specific plans flow up	Leadership team sets general direction; cascades through rest of organization
Contextual	YSI	Presentation and feedback	Leadership creates plan; presents to teams for feedback
Individual	Wainwright	Continuous; focused on established principles	Ongoing process framed around strategic indicators

alterations. Costs are then applied to each component of the plan. An aggregate of these numbers becomes the base projected profit-and-loss statement to which performance will be compared during staff meetings throughout the remainder of the year.

Conceptual DNA: At Johnsonville Sausage, the leadership team examines previous overall company performance as well as the current economic environment, looking for areas of strategic competitive advantage. They develop a preliminary "big picture" plan to provide a general direction for activity. Few, if any, specific goals are included in this plan. The concepts are then presented to the Functional Excellence Teams—the leaders of the major operational divisions of the company—which in turn present them to their departments. Discussions are held throughout the organization on how the concepts might be realized, enhancing employee involvement and commitment. Specific plans are developed at the department level and are cascaded back through each successive level to the leadership team.

Contextual DNA: While the values and overall mission of the organization have been established in team fashion by involving all employees in the YSI organization, it is the management team that largely takes on annual planning. With input from its board of directors, management determines the specific direction for the company to move. Once generated, this information is presented to various employee teams for feedback.

Individual DNA: Wainwright Industries accomplishes its planning process by tracking its five key strategic indicators—safety, employee involvement/satisfaction, customer satisfaction, product quality, and financial performance—to implement long-term strategy. Its overall goals do not change, though the nuances of specific performance levels to be achieved may be altered. For instance, improvement is always monitored, but the number of Continuous Improvement Program projects implemented may rise or fall in a given year.

TEAMWORK

Each of our four companies uses the team concept differently. Table 7 describes how some use teams to solve pressing problems, while others use them to carry out the vision, to create and manage the multiple contexts for performance, or to address a stakeholder concern.

Factual DNA: For the most part, SRC uses a team approach in only one instance—when a unit or facility is in trouble. On the infrequent occasions when this occurs, a team of experts is gathered to go into the troubled area to provide assistance. The team's expertise reflects reliance on data and facts: get in the people who know what they are doing and get the problem fixed. When the problem is resolved, the team dissolves.

Conceptual DNA: Johnsonville Sausage moved from traditional hierarchical management to the use of cross-functional teams in order to transfer responsibility from management to employees. For

Table 7   Teamwork Use and DNA Alignment

DNA Type	Company	Teamwork Use	Manifestation
Factual	Springfield (SRC)	Teams used occasionally for problem solving	Teams consist of content experts; formed to assist failing units
Conceptual	Johnsonville	Teams used extensively to fulfill organizational vision	Formed to ensure individuals can carry out responsibility
Contextual	YSI	Teams used extensively to create organizational structure	Basis of organizational existence
Individual	Wainwright	Teams formed spontaneously to meet customer needs and address other specific issues	All in company referred to as Team Wainwright

instance, when the turnover rate for entry-level factory workers was high, a hiring team made up of individuals from different functional areas was created to develop a new process for hiring. The goal was not to form a team; the goal was to transfer responsibility to those directly affected by the turnover problem. Later, when teams formed in functional work areas, it was not due to a determination to form teams; rather, it was the employees in those areas who began working together in a teamlike manner as they realized they needed each other to be successful.

Contextual DNA: As the overall work context at YSI is one based on teams, teams are employed for just about everything they do. A team determined the mission, products are developed in teams, and problems are addressed by teams. A team elected by the employee-owners determines community involvement. Due to the nature of their work, scientists who develop products are the primary exception to teamwork in this organization. Much of their work is solitary, but even they are members of product development teams—alongside those who will be making, selling, and servicing the product.

Individual DNA: At Wainwright Industries, while associates refer to themselves as "Team Wainwright," teams do not occur purposefully; the focus is on the individual. Most of the time teams are not considered necessary. Spontaneous teams do occur when warranted by a customer's problem. The champion for the customer in question brings together individuals who have an impact on the product. As a group, they clarify the problem and develop and implement a solution. Each team is likely to have a different tenure as well as different member expectations, leadership requirements, and accountabilities. When the problem is resolved, the team dissolves.

PERFORMANCE MANAGEMENT

Every organization has one or more methods to ensure that its employees are performing satisfactorily. For some it is to have a supervisor overseeing work: the supervisor tells workers what to do and then makes sure they do it. Other companies have performance evaluation systems in place: to keep employees accountable for their own performance, they are evaluated once or twice each year. Others use a carrot-and-stick approach: if employees do as they are supposed to, they receive additional compensation or a reward of some sort; if not...

Each DNA type determines a different nuance in the way performance is managed, as illustrated in table 8.

Factual DNA: SRC manages performance through two primary factual mechanisms: the profit-and-loss statement and the bonus system. Each work unit is responsible for achieving production and

Table 8   Performance Management Method and DNA Alignment

DNA Type	Company	Performance Management Method	Manifestation
Factual	Springfield (SRC)	Financial incentive and reinforcement	Conspicuous profit-and-loss statement; performance bonuses
Conceptual	Johnsonville	Reinforcement of personal responsibility	Individual performance contracts with customers
Contextual	YSI	Based on interdependency of individuals	Nonperformance is addressed by the work team since the context is based on relationships
Individual	Wainwright	Based on strategic goals	Continuous Improvement Program; accidents reenacted and shared

financial goals that they were involved in setting at the beginning of each fiscal year. Performance toward these goals is publicly reported during the series of weekly staff meetings. Unit performance is reported at the facility level at the pre–staff meetings. Facility performance is reported to all company managers at the staff meeting. If performance is not up to par, the pressure of having to justify it in front of peers tends to provide employees with the incentive to get performance back on track.

Bonuses are paid quarterly and are based on achievement of critical numbers. Critical numbers accentuate areas where there is an opportunity for improvement over the previous year's performance. For instance, last year there may have been a lower-than-average profit in a particular unit. A specific level of potential improvement will be determined and tracked. If the critical number is not reached, no bonus is paid.

This system also creates a level of peer pressure to keep performance high. Outside influences that affect performance, such as the loss of a major client or a change in the marketplace, are considered a natural part of economic life. If they do affect the critical number, either negatively or positively, no adjustment is made. The market is the market, and, given their history of almost going out of business due to a decline in demand for their product, everyone knows they live or die with the health of the market.

Conceptual DNA: One of the mechanisms Johnsonville Sausage uses to manage performance is the Great Performance Share (GPS). The GPS is a combination performance management, information, and profit-sharing system. It is paid monthly to all members based on performance toward the company's Four Ideal End States, which are based on the concept of personal responsibility: attainment of great products, service, financial results, and employee development.

Each individual or team creates a monthly contract for one or more of the Four Ideal End States. The contract formalizes the level of performance desired; it is posted on the company's computer-based electronic bulletin board. Updates are posted each week indicating what is being done to reach the goal set forth in the contract. At the end of the month, if the contract is completed, the individual or team is eligible for a share of the company profits. (For more information on profit sharing, see the section on compensation on pages 74–76).

Contextual DNA: Performance at YSI is managed within a team milieu. Generally, a team member initially brings a case of nonperformance to the attention of the production coordinator at the business center. Rather than taking responsibility for the issue, the production coordinator brings up the issue with the group involved so they can determine how to address it. Since the team is based on individual relationships, nonperformance is often ignored, as that is perceived to be easier than confronting it.

Each individual does create a performance development plan, which is shared with co-workers for input. The plan, though, is largely focused on individual development.

Individual DNA: At Wainwright Industries, performance is kept totally separate from development. When jobs are open they are posted on a bulletin board, and anyone may apply. Individuals are selected based on their performance. Once in the position, it is presumed that they will perform. The Continuous Improvement Program (CIP) provides individuals with incentive for improvement. Any employee can submit a CIP idea at any time, with little constraint. If the suggestion involves no cost, it can be immediately implemented. If it does involve some cost, the employee works with his or her supervisor to cover the expense.

As a performance development tool, when individuals are involved in a work accident it is reenacted and videotaped. It is then shared at a departmental meeting and narrated by the person involved. In this way all employees learn from the incident.

SUMMARY

Each of our four organizations, as dictated by its specific DNA type, determines the trajectory of its employees' careers—based on performance—differently. Factual DNA–based Springfield Remanufacturing tends to have a very straightforward, matter-of-fact attitude: those not performing to expectations face termination. Conceptual DNA–based Johnsonville Sausage relies on a system created to reinforce individual responsibility, though peers are ready to work with individuals to improve their performance if needed. If this does not work, individuals generally feel pressured by peers to leave the organization.

Table 9 Management Practices and DNA Alignment

DNA Type	Management Practice		
	Planning Process	Teamwork Use	Performance Management Method
Factual	Mechanical, routine	Teams used occasionally for problem solving	Financial incentive and reinforcement
Conceptual	"Fluid drive": concepts cascade down; specific plans flow up	Teams used extensively to fulfill organizational vision	Reinforcement of personal responsibility
Contextual	Presentation and feedback	Teams used extensively to create organizational structure	Based on interdependency of individuals
Individual	Continuous; focused on established principles	Teams formed spontaneously to meet customer needs and address other specific issues	Based on strategic goals

Contextual DNA–based YSI, with its team structure, focuses more on interpersonal team relationships than on specific job skills to solve performance issues. Unless the underlying code of behavior is violated—for instance, if employees are dishonest with their co-workers—there are few terminations. Individual DNA–based Wainwright Industries tracks employees' performance—both good and bad—closely. Great performance is rewarded; but substandard performance, rather than being punished, receives additional attention and support in the form of training. Employee development is paramount.

The three management practices identified are summarized in table 9. Considering your entire organization, which practice do you believe best exemplifies leadership? Does your answer remain the same when you consider only your working department? Is this the same DNA type that you had selected intuitively? If not, does the mis-alignment lead to stress or difficulties in your organization?

Human Resources Practices

Turning from teamwork and performance management, we now look at associated human resources management practices—hiring, compensation, and employee training/development.

HIRING

Table 10 demonstrates the alignment of hiring practices with the various DNA types of our four empowering organizations.

Factual DNA: At Springfield Remanufacturing Corporation (SRC), human resources personnel interview applicants from outside the company. Potential employees are told that 70 percent of the pay is for doing the job, while 30 percent is for learning the business. Despite this forewarning, many new employees find it difficult to adjust to a company that expects every employee to act like an owner. The turnover rate during the first year of employment is about 20 percent; about 90 percent of those who leave do so voluntarily. The primary reason given for their departure is dissatisfaction with the way the business is managed. Workers are not used to having to deal with financial management.

Table 10   Hiring Practice and DNA Alignment

DNA Type	Company	Hiring Practice	Manifestation
Factual	Springfield (SRC)	Contractual agreement	Notification of requirement of financial management; agreement to comply
Conceptual	Johnsonville	Commitment to mission	Hiring done by production workers to get people best able to do job
Contextual	YSI	Contextual fit	Hiring done based on fit with those in organization; skills taught later
Individual	Wainwright	Individual success profile	Hiring based on individual talents as foundation for focused skills

Unless there is no one with the technical capacity for the job, SRC promotes only from within. All jobs in the organization are posted, and a management committee interviews all applicants. Other employees can provide input, but management makes the final decisions. The job interview process can be quite intensive, at times involving Human Resources, plant management, and other workers who will be directly affected by the potential employee.

Conceptual DNA: At one point, Johnsonville Sausage had a high turnover rate for entry-level employees. After an examination of the situation, it was found that employees thought the human resources department was only hiring "warm bodies" for production positions. As a result, the current employees were not helping new employees learn their jobs, which then resulted in many newly hired employees leaving after a short period.

The managers decided to transfer responsibility to those most affected by the turnover. Each work area designates an employee to be responsible for hiring. He or she then forms a hiring team that meets regularly with a human resources professional to learn how to do hiring.

Every job opening is posted, and any current employee may apply for the job. The team or work area hiring the individual creates its own process for determining who will be hired. Most often this takes the form of a group interview including team members and internal customers who will use the services of the position. All members of the team have an equal voice. The person selected for the job is the one considered most qualified to do it; it is his or her responsibility to gain the knowledge to do the job *prior* to applying. If no one is qualified, the team will look outside the company.

Contextual DNA: At YSI, the hiring process is designed to ensure, as much as possible, that a new person will fit into the company. In the production area, workers may start in either part-time or temporary positions. If there is a good fit with the organization, they will be moved into full-time positions when they become available.

Often, in hiring people from outside the company, direct experience or even job skills appear to be irrelevant. The more pertinent hiring criteria appear to be fitting in and the ability to learn as opposed to possession of a specific set of skills.

Individual DNA: Wainwright Industries uses a behavior-based targeted selection process. They have identified specific characteristics of individuals who succeed at the company, such as an entrepreneurial spirit, and they target hires who fit that profile. Individuals can be promoted even if they do not have the skills in advance; the company will train them. The underlying belief is a focus on learning to allow all persons to use their talents and become the best they can be. Over 60 percent of the company's employees have been promoted at least once; some have been promoted numerous times.

COMPENSATION

Creating a compensation system to reinforce the type of performance desired presents a challenge for all organizations. In his article on performance management, Kerr (1975) suggests that it is folly to reward A while hoping for B. In other words, the compensation system should reward the performance being sought as opposed to simply rewarding an employee for being present, as many compensation systems do. As indicated in table 11, our four organizations appear to have figured this out.

Though each of the four organizations has a somewhat different compensation system, all four have a profit-sharing plan that pays out at least quarterly. It is likely that this element is in common due to their common focus on empowerment.

Factual DNA: SRC's base-wage system is traditional, in that employees are paid on an hourly basis and the supervisor determines pay increases. Bonuses in the form of profit sharing are provided for all employees based on the achievement of critical numbers—set by management and measured and reported to management on a weekly basis—as well as through the fulfillment of the financial plan. The profits are shared, with 18 percent of base pay going to managers and 15 percent of base pay to others. The process is easy to track, and each employee knows if he or she will get the bonus by examining the results identified in the weekly meetings.

Conceptual DNA: Johnsonville Sausage, the company that focuses on personal responsibility, has a results-based pay system that provides hourly employees with control over their own pay increases. They can receive a pay increase as soon as they demonstrate to coworkers that they can perform well enough to achieve the expected results.

The Great Performance Share (GPS) system provides all Johnsonville members with a share of the profits based on attainment of

Table 11   Compensation Basis and DNA Alignment

DNA Type	Company	Compensation Basis	Manifestation
Factual	Springfield (SRC)	Achievement	Traditional hourly pay system; profit-sharing bonus based on achieving management's set goals
Conceptual	Johnsonville	Commitment	System rewards individual taking responsibility; profit sharing based on performance toward ideal end states
Contextual	YSI	Engagement	Two pay grades, with all paid same within each grade; all paid hourly rate; equal profit sharing for all
Individual	Wainwright	Scaled equality	Two pay grades; increases in range based on time in grade; equal percentage share of profits for all

individual or team-based contracts connected to the Four Ideal End States. If employees choose not to take responsibility for improvement, they receive no portion of the company profits. The GPS averages 10–15 percent in addition to base wages for hourly paid members and 15–30 percent in addition to salary for all others. The specific amount is determined by how profitable the organization is each month.

Contextual DNA: YSI has a "broadband" pay system for all production jobs. There are two pay grades: one covers most production positions; the other is for jobs that require higher technical skill. In an egalitarian move, all employees are paid on an hourly basis—production, support, and leadership alike. Profit sharing is conducted quarterly, and by a vote of all employees profits are shared equally by all employees regardless of position.

Individual DNA: At stakeholder-based Wainwright Industries, each job has a pay grade. An employee will receive three equal pay increases in his or her grade, one every six months until the top of the grade is reached. There are then no pay increases until a new pay grade is attained. The pay system is not tied to performance; each individual is treated the same: up to 25 percent of profits are shared evenly on a quarterly basis and put into a 401(k) account for each employee.

EMPLOYEE TRAINING/DEVELOPMENT

The four organizations featured in this study all focus on empowering employees; training or the creation of learning systems and employee development are critical for them. Learning is emphasized in several of these organizations. A training system puts the responsibility for content and approach in the hands of the trainer; learning, on the other hand, is the responsibility of the employee. A learning approach is more conducive to empowerment. Table 12 shows the alignment between each organization's DNA and its development programs.

Factual DNA: From a career-planning standpoint, Springfield Remanufacturing provides opportunities for growth, and it requires that all employees participate. Career planning is done annually by everybody in the plant; working with their supervisors, individuals look at yearly and longer-term goals and develop plans to reach them. Tuition for formal educational programs is reimbursable. Skill

Table 12   Employee Training/Development and DNA Alignment

DNA Type	Company	Employee Training/ Development	Manifestation
Factual	Springfield (SRC)	Required; all individuals must have development plans	Individual career plans required of all employees; emphasis on formal classes at educational institutions
Conceptual	Johnsonville	Customized; individuals can have development plans created to fit their individual styles and needs	Full-time member development resource person available to help member take responsibility for own development; learning may be in classroom setting or not
Contextual	YSI	Mutually developed among leadership and team members	Formal development plan revisited twice per year; learning system designed by a team
Individual	Wainwright	Self-determined; individuals select learning opportunities based on personal interest	Each individual has a development plan; financial assistance available for tuition whether class is work related or not

enhancement opportunities as well as management-focused learning are available to those who want to take advantage of them.

Conceptual DNA: While Johnsonville Sausage employees are responsible for their own development, the company puts in place systems to assist them. For instance, they have a member development center equipped with computers, a library, and meeting space. They also have a full-time member development staff person able to help individuals in thinking through their learning plans.

Other programs, like the Member Interaction Program, give every person in the company a chance to spend a day working with anyone else. After spending a day with a salesperson, for example, employees—in Manufacturing, in Billing, or in any other department—begin to see how what they do affects Sales. Their job begins to take on a whole new meaning. Many learning opportunities are provided in-house, and employees attending formal education programs are paid in advance through the company's Continuing Education Fund. If the class is not completed, he or she reimburses the company for the tuition.

Contextual DNA: At YSI, the learning system was designed by its Council on Employee Development (COED). Each employee is part of the Performance Agreement and Development Plan, which covers accountability, short-term goals, long-term goals, and individual learning units. The development plan is a living document that is officially revisited twice a year. In addition to identifying what performance goals they agree to, employee-owners individually select several other members of the company who see their work on a regular basis to review their performance.

The performance agreement is then used as the basis for a conversation regarding development. A specific development plan, with related coursework, is written out and signed by the employee-owner and his or her leader.

Individual DNA: Wainwright views learning and development as the keys to organizational success. All employees have a performance development plan in place, which replaced the old performance appraisal that required supervisors to assess employees. Now twice each year supervisors meet with each employee individually to review what he or she has done well in the past six months and to choose two areas that the employee can further develop and that will support the overall goals of the company. These are maintained as development goals for the next six months. Supervisors don't appraise the past; they develop a plan so that the individual can determine where he or she wants to go. Performance deficiencies are not handled at these planning meetings; that work is done as soon as performance problems are identified.

Employees have the opportunity to continually work on their interpersonal job-specific skills to help them fulfill their development plans. The company spends approximately 7 percent of its payroll on training and development.

SUMMARY

We can see that while each organization banks on continued growth and development of its employees and staff, they all provide resources and have expectations in line with their DNA. The learning and development systems are in place to support the goals and contracts employees have with their company.

Table 13 summarizes the three human resources practices identified. Considering your entire organization, which do you believe best exemplifies human resources? Does your answer remain the same when you consider only your working department? Is this the same DNA type that you had intuitively selected? If not, does the misalignment lead to stress or difficulties in your organization?

Table 13 Human Resources Practices and DNA Alignment

| | Human Resources Practice | | |
DNA Type	Hiring Practice	Compensation Basis	Employee Training/ Development
Factual	Contractual agreement	Achievement	Required; all individuals must have development plans
Conceptual	Commitment to mission	Commitment	Customized; individuals can have development plans created to fit their individual styles and needs
Contextual	Contextual fit	Engagement	Mutually developed among leadership and team members
Individual	Individual success profile	Scaled equality	Self-determined; individuals select learning opportunities based on personal interest

Everyday Cultural Practices

In earlier chapters we indicated the ways in which our four DNA types lead to distinct leadership, managerial, human resources, and other practices. Yet, we know that all organizational systems are interrelated. For example, individual employees experience and have to manage conflicts during hiring or compensation discussions or have to make decisions involving leadership concerns.

In this chapter, we examine the various factors that make up the culture of an organization. We begin with a look at decision-making approaches and then move on to the shaping of interpersonal relationships, change processes, and the view of profits.

DECISION MAKING

While there are many circumstances that affect how and when decisions are made, our four organizations exhibit basic patterns in their approach to decision making. Table 14 illustrates the variety of approaches as they are determined by the four DNA types.

Factual DNA: At SRC there is a clear delineation of levels of decision-making accountability. Executives are responsible for deter-

Table 14   Decision-Making Approach and DNA Alignment

DNA Type	Company	Decision-Making Approach	Manifestation
Factual	Springfield (SRC)	Accountability	Executive: strategic investments, new business; management: operations, new-business recommendations, financial results tracking, plant systems development; employees: day-to-day performance and improvement
Conceptual	Johnsonville	Personal responsibility leading to joint responsibility	Those affected/involved resolve issues
Contextual	YSI	Issue generated	Day-to-day issues; production workers bring in process/product engineers to work through issues collaboratively
Individual	Wainwright	Operational	Day-to-day operating decisions made by operators and production employees even if cost involved; system changes made by management

mining the strategic direction and for deciding whether to undertake new investments, and they have final approval on the creation of new businesses. Managers are accountable for the operations of the facilities, for knowing at all times how their unit is performing, for recommending new businesses based on their experience with customers, for tracking financial results, and for developing plant systems. Employees are accountable for day-to-day production as well as their own performance. They also have the opportunity to make suggestions for process improvement.

Conceptual DNA: At Johnsonville Sausage, employees extend the concept of personal responsibility to joint responsibility. A project initiator, or an employee who identifies a problem, has responsibility for bringing together those involved or affected by the issue in order to investigate and develop solutions. If capital expenditure is involved, this ad hoc team prepares a capital request and submits it to a capital expenditure team. If the issue has been thoroughly explained and justified, and if there are funds available, the capital expenditure team generally approves the request. If the expenditure team feels the justification is not complete, questions are generated to clarify their concerns and the request is referred back to the initiating team for further consideration. A full explanation is provided in the rare case when a request is turned down.

Contextual DNA: At YSI, an employee demonstrating strong interest, or by request, takes the lead on an issue, investigates it, and develops solutions by bringing together those involved or affected. When it is production members who initiate a change, they bring in resource people such as process or product engineers to work with them through an issue. While the approach is similar to that at Johnsonville, the focus here is more on the importance of team collaboration in problem solving and decision making.

Individual DNA: Individual production employees make the day-to-day operating decisions at Wainwright Industries. Although as a common courtesy leadership is generally informed, employees are not required to check with anyone to implement an improvement, even if there is a cost involved. Management, though, makes decisions involving changes in work systems, as these will affect more than one individual and will relate to the defined governance process.

INTERPERSONAL RELATIONSHIPS

Table 15 describes how conflicts in interpersonal relationships are managed based on the organization's dominant DNA.

Factual DNA: When individuals are hired at Springfield Remanufacturing, they are required to sign a formal statement that they will address any personal conflicts directly with the other person(s) involved. Management does not want to deal with such issues. The statement is meant to be taken seriously; in the rare instance when an interpersonal conflict is not resolved, all involved employees face termination.

Conceptual DNA: At Johnsonville Sausage, individuals are expected to take personal responsibility for their performance. This includes their relationships with co-workers. If there is an interpersonal conflict, it is expected that those involved will deal with it themselves. If this approach proves unsuccessful, individuals receive coaching from management. If that is also unsuccessful, third-party facilitators are brought in to assist in the process.

Contextual DNA: Since employees at YSI spend so much of their time working in teams, interpersonal relationships at this company are critical. Employees take classes to learn how to resolve conflicts, should they occur. However, when they do occur, conflicts are often more likely to be ignored than to be resolved, as they are contrary to the organizational focus. The team approach seems to have led to a "go along and get along" attitude.

Individual DNA: Most of the work at Wainwright Industries is performed by employees working alone or in small groups, with the focus of the group generally being a machine requiring attention. Interpersonal relationships are thus largely framed around the work that is done. As a result, there is little conflict in this organization.

Table 15   Interpersonal Relationship Approach and DNA Alignment

DNA Type	Company	Interpersonal Relationship Approach	Manifestation
Factual	Springfield (SRC)	Formalized	Employees sign a statement agreeing to address issues with others; failure to resolve conflicts is grounds for termination
Conceptual	Johnsonville	Reliability based	Individuals rely on one another to perform; coach works with individuals to work out issues
Contextual	YSI	Interdependent	Management assumes all will get along, but trains employees in conflict resolution; may or may not address issues as they arise for fear of harming relationships
Individual	Wainwright	Networked	Very little conflict occurs; no formal mechanism; focus on individual, who works with others when needed but is largely independent

Table 16　Change Process Purpose and DNA Alignment

DNA Type	Company	Change Process Purpose	Manifestation
Factual	Springfield (SRC)	To achieve goals	Initiated at plant or individual level, based on reducing costs or generating new business
Conceptual	Johnsonville	To eliminate the gap between practice and driving concept	Individuals may initiate operational changes; strategic changes generally initiated by CEO as company visionary
Contextual	YSI	To provide for collaborative responsiveness	Customers request product or change; person receiving request spearheads change
Individual	Wainwright	To address stakeholder issues	Employees, in teams, address opportunities for improvement based on customer requests/demands and, as individuals, address concerns related to safety

CHANGE PROCESSES

Table 16 shows how change is initiated and implemented according to the organization's dominant DNA. (Major organizational change issues will be addressed in chapter 11, "The Clash of DNA.")

Factual DNA: At SRC, change is generally initiated at the plant or individual level and is focused almost exclusively on the impact to the bottom line. For example, an employee may have an idea on how to reduce the amount of scrap generated in a process, thereby decreasing the cost of the process.

If a suggestion for change will have an impact outside the scope of the employee's work, it is brought to the fore during the annual planning process and may be incorporated for the current year or be considered as a contingency. Contingencies are ideas for business growth developed to the point of implementation and then held until there is a need to expand the business.

Conceptual DNA: At Johnsonville Sausage, change is written into the company's mission statement. As each individual is responsible for his or her own performance, anyone may initiate a change, with help from the affected area. For example, a packaging employee with an idea for a product improvement might be directed to Sales to move her idea forward.

This approach largely holds true for day-to-day or operational issues; however, the owner initiates most strategic changes, such as when he or she senses a trend toward stability in the organization—which tends to lead to complacency. At Johnsonville, some level of chaos or urgency is considered desirable to help keep employees focused on the job at hand.

Contextual DNA: YSI customers requesting a product improvement or enhancement initiate most organizational changes. In keeping with the collaborative approach, the person receiving the customer's request forms an ad hoc team of all those who will be affected. When the issue has been resolved, the team dissolves.

Changes in internal systems are often initiated from within the department and arise when there is incongruency between practice and process. For instance, on a practical matter such as the assembly of a component, where an engineer has developed the specifications but production employees find the process cumbersome, change is initiated by the employees, who request that the engineer meet with them to review the process.

Table 17   View of Profits and DNA Alignment

DNA Type	Company	View of Profits	Rationale
Factual	Springfield (SRC)	Reason for being	To ensure that the doors will never close
Conceptual	Johnsonville	Reinforcement of driving idea	To motivate employees to take responsibility
Contextual	YSI	To allow the organization to continue	Necessary to continue team-based management
Individual	Wainwright	To provide proof of value	If all else is done well, profits will follow

Individual DNA: At Wainwright Industries, change is initiated in two ways. One is through a customer request or concern that leads to the only visible use of teamwork at the company. All stakeholders who will be affected by the change work together to resolve the issue and improve customer satisfaction. Once this focused effort leads to a solution, the team is dissolved.

The other way change occurs is when employees see opportunities for improvement in safety, employee involvement/satisfaction, or product quality. The Continuous Improvement Program provides an institutional process for eliciting change. Individuals are encouraged to implement changes and to submit their ideas to a quarterly drawing for monetary rewards.

VIEW OF PROFITS

Surprisingly, even the ways in which profits are viewed vary from organization to organization based on their DNA, as illustrated in table 17.

Factual DNA: SRC developed its management model when it was part of a much larger organization that was rapidly spinning into bankruptcy. The plant managers engineered a buyout of the facility. As a result, their view of profits is to ensure that the doors will never close and that employees will never lose their jobs. Profits are why they are in business.

Conceptual DNA: At Johnsonville Sausage, the primary purpose for achieving profitability is to ensure the continuation of the business. Nearly as important, however, is reinforcing the concept of individuals taking responsibility for their own performance—which is reinforced through their profit-sharing program. For the employees also, then, profits have become a reason to do what they do.

Contextual DNA: Without profits, organizations cannot continue to stay in business. At YSI the company also must have profits to be able to continue its social experiment implementing McGregor's theory of industrial democracy.

Individual DNA: Wainwright Industries also sees profits as critical, but rather than purposefully striving for them, they view profits as inevitable if all else is done well. Profits provide the proof of the value of the organization and the individuals in it.

SUMMARY

Each of these practices reflects a distinct culture. As we have seen, how each culture manifests itself will vary based on the DNA of the organization. (The cultures we have described are consistent with the basic patterns of broader cultural foundations as identified by Pepper [1942], Detienne [1996], and others. Pepper's four "world hypotheses" echo our four DNA types; they also allow you to extend your observations of the everyday cultural practices noted here to larger themes, expanding them, perhaps, into a liberal art.)

Table 18 summarizes the cultural issues identified in this chapter. Considering your entire organization, which do you believe best

Table 18   Everyday Cultural Practices and DNA Alignment

| | Everyday Cultural Practice | | | |
DNA Type	Decision-Making Approach	Interpersonal Relationship Approach	Performance Management Method	View of Profits
Factual	Accountability	Formalized	To achieve goals	Reason for being
Conceptual	Personal responsibility leading to joint responsibility	Reliability based	To eliminate the gap between practice and driving concept	Reinforcement of driving idea
Contextual	Issue generated	Interdependent	To provide for collaborative responsiveness	To allow the organization to continue
Individual	Operational	Networked	To address stakeholder issues	To provide proof of value

exemplifies your organizational culture? Does your answer remain the same when you consider only your working department? Is this the same DNA type that you had intuitively selected? If not, does the incongruency lead to stress or difficulties in your organization?

10

Attaining Alignment

On a personal level, the concept of alignment brings forth many associations from our memories and experiences. It suggests a kind of wholeness or integrity that allows for and shapes one's individuality. There are many ways in which we attempt to create alignments in our lives. We speak of individuals as "whole persons." We identify their learning styles in ways that support alternative models of accomplishing a common educational goal. We identify integrity as a focus that relates to values. We can also focus on the achievement of integrity as it relates to organizational practices. Organizations' alignments are the foundation for their wholeness, their integrity, and their effectiveness.

WHAT DOES ALIGNMENT LOOK LIKE?

When you ask executives about the future of their organizations, they might think in terms of interlocking circles or path diagrams or other images, even a hierarchical pattern, demonstrating that individuals have different pictures in their heads about relationships among parts and even what constitutes a part. The actual presentation of alignment or integrity can take different forms, and this is especially true in the spirit of globalization and the impact of information technologies. Boundaries are more and more permeable and have less salience; horizontal patterns coexist with vertical ones; temporary and more permanent elements are jointly involved in project management; and both tacit/intuitive and explicit knowledge are engaged, as well as more generic and local understandings, as the turbulence of markets holds sway. So, given such complexity, what does it mean to talk about alignment?

While the presentation of organizational alignment may take very different forms, we suggest that the early Greek notions of balance, proportion, and harmony have pertinence. We are looking not for sameness, but for patterns that fit, while recognizing the systemic individuality of either the individual or organization. In individual cases, this may relate to demographic or cultural differences; for organizations, we suggest, it relates to their DNA.

It is also critical to recognize that there are other ways to communicate complexities outside the more linear or horizontal, which capture organizational patterns that suggest novel relationships among the parts. Andrew Pickering's (1995) notions of "interactive stabilization" or "intertwining," and Collins and Kusch's (1998) ideas around "cascading," and "conjugating," for example, suggest alignment patterns for our conceptual DNA–based organization, in the same way that the hierarchy does for the factual DNA–based alternative.

In spite of these alternative patterns and ways of talking about them, what we present below to discuss alignment is a traditional grid form. It is important not to confuse the grid presentation of the ideas and the integrities of those factors in each column with the consequences of their "hanging together." The forms of the organizations will differ substantially, even though our way of presenting these differences does not.

In table 19, we chart the organizational practices we have identified—leadership, management, human resources, and cultural—and their DNA alignment as complementary, which we believe is essential for organizational effectiveness.

ORGANIZATIONAL PRACTICES AND DNA ALIGNMENT

You can compare any practice in the left-hand column in table 19 and see how it relates effectively to the dominant DNA and how it differs from the manifestation of that practice in the other DNA types. You can see as well the different logic in play within each organizational type.

Organizational effectiveness demands that practices be aligned. For example, it does not make sense to use a factual DNA-based hiring practice and a compensation plan based on conceptual DNA. If you hire on the basis of a contracted agreement, then the issue is whether the employee has performed as expected—not his or her commitment to the organization's vision or the quality of the parties' engagements with each other in joint projects. Similarly, if hiring is based on contextual fit, then individual achievement would not be a valid basis for assessment, but the effectiveness of joint engagements would be.

We are not suggesting that an organization should not demonstrate traits of other, subsidiary, DNA types. It is highly unlikely that any organization could be perfectly aligned and totally one-dimensional. At some level you would expect that a person hired in a factual DNA-based company would display personal commitment and that a person hired in a contextual DNA-based one would demonstrate a desire for personal achievement, even though these are not the prime touchstones

Table 19   Organizational Practices and DNA Alignment

	Leadership Practices		
DNA Type	Mission Purpose	Governance Structure	Leadership Style
Factual	Specify the goal	Hierarchical	Transactional; responsible for regulating the work of the organization
Conceptual	Set the vision	Concentric	Transformational; reframing issues to address organizational idea
Contextual	Provide for linked foundations	Federated (multiple centers of leadership)	Adaptive
Individual	Identify indicators of success	Federated democracy; loosely woven	Interactive

	Management Practices		
DNA Type	Planning Purpose	Teamwork Use	Performance Management Method
Factual	Mechanical, routine	Teams used occasionally for problem solving	Financial incentive and reinforcement
Conceptual	"Fluid drive": concepts cascade down; specific plans flow up	Teams used extensively to fulfill organizational vision	Reinforcement of personal responsibility
Contextual	Presentation and feedback	Teams used extensively to create organizational structure	Based on interdependency of individuals
Individual	Continuous; focused on established principles	Teams formed spontaneously to meet customer needs and address other specific issues	Based on strategic goals

Table 19   Organizational Practices and DNA Alignment (continued)

DNA Type	Human Resources Practices		
	Hiring Practice	Compensation Basis	Employee Training/ Development
Factual	Contractual agreement	Achievement	Required; all individuals must have development plans
Conceptual	Commitment to mission	Commitment	Customized; individuals can have development plans created to fit their individual styles and needs
Contextual	Contextual fit	Engagement	Mutually developed among leadership and team members
Individual	Individual success profile	Scaled equality	Self-determined; individuals select learning opportunities based on personal interest

DNA Type	Everyday Cultural Practices			
	Decision-Making Approach	Interpersonal Relationship Approach	Performance Management Method	View of Profits
Factual	Accountability	Formalized	To achieve goals	Reason for being
Conceptual	Personal responsibility leads to joint responsibility	Reliability based	To eliminate gap between practice and driving concept	Reinforcement of driving idea
Contextual	Issue generated	Interdependent	To provide for collaborative responsiveness	To allow the organization to continue
Individual	Operational	Networked	To address stakeholder issues	To provide proof of value

for such organizations. To the degree that there is some concern for the attainment of an outcome or a definition of a practice outside the directives of the dominant DNA of the organization, such outcome or practice should be redefined so that it "fits."

Using the examples above, commitment in a factual DNA enviroment might be defined as an employee's focus on, and sustained attention to, the organization's goals; personal achievement in a contextual DNA setting could be met by providing leadership to multiple teams and by seeing one's growth as a fusion, linking together disparate elements for more creative possibilities. In this and in all cases, the dominant DNA provides the touchstone for the actions that ensue and the ways in which we frame them as challenges and accomplishments.

ASSESSMENT—DETERMINING YOUR ORGANIZATIONAL DNA

At the beginning of this book, we asked you to use your intuition in determining your organizational DNA. Here, as promised, is a tool to assist you.

Directions

Over the next few pages, brief descriptions of organizational practices from each DNA type are provided. As you read each of these descriptors, place a check mark by the one that best describes: (1) your organization as a whole, and (2) your functional unit or department.

This information will be used as you determine your own organizational alignment. Are specific practices best designed for your overall organizational DNA? Are practices at the organizational level in line with those at the unit level? In chapter 11 we will discuss ways for you to work toward alignment.

LEADERSHIP PRACTICES

Org.	Unit	Mission
☐	☐	*Factual:* If present in written form at all, the mission of the factual DNA–based organization is very direct. Specific goals are stated, and processes for performance and mechanisms for measurement are predetermined.
☐	☐	*Conceptual:* The mission is presented as a focused statement of ideals specifically formed around a concept or idea. The statement is broad enough to allow individual interpretation around a general theme.
☐	☐	*Contextual:* The contextual DNA–based mission lays out a structure for interwoven relationships, both internal and external, in the organization.
☐	☐	*Individual:* Projected indicators of performance provide a touchstone for keeping everyone headed in the same general direction. Specific activities are designed along the way.

Org.	Unit	Governance Structure
☐	☐	*Factual:* Hierarchy is the structure of choice in a factual DNA–based organization.
☐	☐	*Conceptual:* Structure itself keeps individuals moving toward the same idea that forms the basis of the organization.
☐	☐	*Contextual:* The structure determines how people interrelate with one another. It may comprise teams, a matrix, or some other format that allows multiple centers of power and influence.

☐ ☐ **Individual:** The structure here is loosely woven. Individuals have a great deal of autonomy but also an allegiance to the main organization. A familiar example would be a university, where professors are in departments, which are in schools, which are in the university, yet the professors remain relatively autonomous.

Org.	Unit	Leadership Style

☐ ☐ **Factual:** In the factual DNA–based organization, leadership is responsible for regulating the work environment and for ensuring adherence to the rules established.

☐ ☐ **Conceptual:** Leadership here is often charismatic. It is the role of the leader to reframe issues so that they are in alignment with the original overriding organizational concept.

☐ ☐ **Contextual:** Leadership responds to the issues that arise from internal and external environments composed of various stakeholders.

☐ ☐ **Individual:** Harmony is important in the organization focused on individuals. Leaders act to clarify and resolve issues.

Leadership Practices Tally

Organization: ___ Factual ___ Conceptual ___ Contextual ___ Individual

Unit: ___ Factual ___ Conceptual ___ Contextual ___ Individual

MANAGEMENT PRACTICES

Org.	Unit	Planning
☐	☐	**Factual:** In the factual DNA–based organization, planning is accomplished through a regularly established routine and completed in a similar manner each time it is done.
☐	☐	**Conceptual:** In the conceptual DNA–based organization, the planning process is flexible and fluid, adapting to the current issues affecting the organization.
☐	☐	**Contextual:** Leadership in the contextual DNA–based organization likely directs the planning process and makes the final decisions on a plan after receiving feedback from various subgroups.
☐	☐	**Individual:** Planning is a continuous process at the individual DNA–based organization. Since projected indicators are selected in the mission, individuals can refer back to them on an as-needed basis to adapt their own actions.

Org.	Unit	Teamwork
☐	☐	**Factual:** Teams are used only when there is a strong need to have a problem resolved. The team would generally consist of only those directly affected by the problem or those who could provide a level of expertise.
☐	☐	**Conceptual:** Teams are used wherever they might be helpful in fulfilling the major idea around which the organization is framed.

☐ ☐   **Contextual:** A relational mechanism such as teams is used to support the framework of the organization. If the context is one that requires problem solving, teams are used extensively.

☐ ☐   **Individual:** The individual who identifies an issue or problem may bring together resources functioning as a team to deal with it. Once the issue is resolved, this team will dissolve back to individuals working independently.

Org.	Unit	Performance Management

☐ ☐   **Factual:** Performance is expected at the factual DNA-based organization. If it is not achieved, financial rewards may be withheld or the employee may be terminated.

☐ ☐   **Conceptual:** Performance management systems are improvised to support the major idea around which the organization is framed.

☐ ☐   **Contextual:** Individuals write performance plans that link them to the contextual framework of the organization.

☐ ☐   **Individual:** The performance indicators as identified in the mission provide the metrics by which individual performance is measured.

Management Practices Tally

Organization: ___ *Factual* ___ *Conceptual* ___ *Contextual* ___ *Individual*

Unit: ___ *Factual* ___ *Conceptual* ___ *Contextual* ___ *Individual*

HUMAN RESOURCES PRACTICES

Org.	Unit	Hiring
☐	☐	*Factual:* The employment contract between the organization and the individual is straightforward: X amount of wages will be provided for X amount of labor.
☐	☐	*Conceptual:* In the concept-based organization, individuals are selected who exemplify an understanding of, and commitment to, the organizational ideal.
☐	☐	*Contextual:* Personal fit into the work context is of primary importance. Employees may be selected for hire if they fit with the organization even though they do not yet have the specific skills for the job.
☐	☐	*Individual:* Potential employees are screened for predetermined key characteristics that ensure they will thrive in this environment.

Org.	Unit	Compensation
☐	☐	*Factual:* In a factual DNA–based organization employees are compensated based on their achievement. Their performance is evaluated, and the best performers are more highly compensated.
☐	☐	*Conceptual:* The company is likely to have a unique compensation system that reinforces the vision or idea around which the company is formed.
☐	☐	*Contextual:* Engagement or levels of involvement are rewarded in the contextual DNA–based organization.

☐   ☐   *Individual:* It is likely that all employees are rewarded equally—that is, in proportion to their responsibility. Therefore, all individuals in one class receive roughly equivalent compensation.

Org.	Unit	Employee Training/Development

☐   ☐   *Factual:* If employee development is important in the factual DNA–based organization, all employees may be required to participate. They likely have to write a development plan and keep it on file. The plans may be reviewed on a regular basis to compare actual development to the plan.

☐   ☐   *Conceptual:* In the conceptual DNA–based organization the employee development program is customized to fit the major idea around which the company is formed. Development likely is not required, as it is assumed that all employees want to learn in order to better achieve the organization's goals.

☐   ☐   *Contextual:* Development opportunities are offered to reinforce the central needs and foci of the organization. Employees may be required to attend these sessions. If individuals have development plans, co-workers likely have input into each other's development plans.

☐   ☐   *Individual:* A system is in place whereby employees may choose to develop themselves, but it is not mandatory. Employees are likely rewarded for development.

Human Resources Practices Tally

Organization: ___ *Factual* ___ *Conceptual* ___ *Contextual* ___ *Individual*

Unit: ___ *Factual* ___ *Conceptual* ___ *Contextual* ___ *Individual*

EVERYDAY CULTURAL PRACTICES

Org.	Unit	Decision Making
☐	☐	*Factual:* The critical component of decision making in a factual DNA–based environment is to provide a strong sense of accountability. The hierarchy indicates which individuals are responsible for which decisions.
☐	☐	*Conceptual:* The individual responsible for an issue identifies an area where a decision needs to be made. The individual then engages others who will be affected by the decision to work together to resolve the issue in alignment with the framing idea.
☐	☐	*Contextual:* Those affected by an issue are brought together by whoever identifies the problem. Resource people are brought in to assist in their areas of expertise. The usual approach is to form a collaborative group to resolve the issue.
☐	☐	*Individual:* Decision making is individual based. If an individual sees a problem, he or she may resolve it. Others are informed as an act of courtesy or are engaged as a resource if the individual is unclear on how to move forward.

Org.	Unit	Interpersonal Relationships
☐	☐	*Factual:* Relationships in the factual DNA–based organization are formal and dependent largely on mutual need for achieving personal success.
☐	☐	*Conceptual:* Interpersonal relationships are generated among those who can be relied on to work toward the original or evolving organizational concept.

		Contextual: Interdependency is the driving force. Employees have ongoing relationships across departmental and perhaps even divisional boundaries.
☐	☐	**Individual:** In the individual DNA–based organization interpersonal relationships are chosen based on personal affinity.

Org.	Unit	Change Processes
☐	☐	**Factual:** Change will be initiated in the factual DNA-based organization when there is a gap between the goals of the organization and actual performance.
☐	☐	**Conceptual:** A perceived difference between current practice and the ideal set forth in the company's vision statement will lead to change. This will not be based on a specific goal, but rather on the adherence to an idea.
☐	☐	**Contextual:** Change occurs as a collaborative response to an external request made by customers or other stakeholders.
☐	☐	**Individual:** In the individual DNA–based organization, a massive shift in the market or the needs of individual stakeholders will be the primary driving factor for change.

Org.	Unit	View of Profits
☐	☐	**Factual:** Profits are the reason for being. Without profit, there is no reason to exist. (*Note:* in nonprofit organizations "profit" may be substituted with "financial goals" or an alternative metric.)

☐   ☐   *Conceptual:* At the conceptual DNA–based organization, the attainment of profits reinforces the value of the central idea.

☐   ☐   *Contextual:* Profits exist to allow the organization, and the context, to stay in existence.

☐   ☐   *Individual:* Profits provide a proof of the value of the individual in the organization.

Everyday Cultural Practices Tally

Organization: ___ *Factual* ___ *Conceptual* ___ *Contextual* ___ *Individual*

Unit: ___ *Factual* ___ *Conceptual* ___ *Contextual* ___ *Individual*

SCORING YOUR ORGANIZATIONAL DNA

Now that you have completed each section, you can total your overall points. The first score sheet is for your organization; the second is for your unit within the organization.

The column in the organization score sheet with the highest overall score should best reflect your organization's DNA. While this is not a scientific instrument, and your scores are based on

ORGANIZATION DNA SCORE SHEET

Organization	DNA Type			
	Factual	*Conceptual*	*Contextual*	*Individual*
Leadership Practice				
Management Practice				
Human Resources Practice				
Everyday Cultural Practice				
Total				

your perception of your organization, we anticipate that the scores will ring true—that is, they will match the intuitive selection you made after studying the organizational examples in part 1.

You have read a good deal about organizational DNA since making an initial intuitive determination of your organization's DNA. If the result here does not match your intuitive selection,

UNIT DNA SCORE SHEET

Unit	DNA Type			
	Factual	*Conceptual*	*Contextual*	*Individual*
Leadership Practice				
Management Practice				
Human Resources Practice				
Everyday Cultural Practice				
Total				

why do you believe this is the case? Which DNA do you now believe is most descriptive of your organization? Why?

A "perfect" score in any column on either score sheet is unlikely. Practices on the organization and unit levels may have developed based on examples from other companies or based on the DNA style of a specific manager that is not in tune with the logic of the organization. You might ask yourself what is entailed in creating such alignment and how the redefinition of your management practices might enhance organizational performance.

The column in the unit score sheet with the highest score should best reflect your unit's DNA. Remember, this is not a scientific instrument; it is based on your perception of your unit. Does the finding ring true for your unit? Does it match the intuitive selection you made after reading the organizational examples? If this total does not match your intuitive selection, why do you believe this is the case?

Is there a difference between your unit's DNA and that of the organization? What does that suggest to you as you reflect on the differences between them? Are there differences between your unit and another unit, and does this cause stress, create misperceptions, or allow other problems to form? Identification of these differences is the first step in understanding and resolving them by aligning DNA types.

FACING DNA MISALIGNMENT

Most of the challenges organizations face are tactical; that is, they are embedded in everyday practices and they require the creative use of resources to manage the various practices. As well, strategic issues involving the articulation of activities, including their considered continuation or the introduction of new activities, often place organizations somewhere between two or more structural elements. We call this the "in-between."

Functioning in the "In-Between"

When you are dealing with uncertainties and managing highly turbulent and complex systems, you are often just trying to put things back on track, that is, trying to align your practices from the space in-between. This space is not typically presented in the management literature.

As an exercise, go back now and look at the spaces in-between the thirteen processes located within each DNA type column in table 19, "Organizational Practices and DNA Alignment," on pages 94–95. Such consideration will emphasize the challenges involved as you try to create a "whole organization" and suggest a variety of questions. For example, in a factual DNA–based organization,

◊ What does your experience tell you about how individuals in various hierarchical positions relate to the mechanical routines evident in the planning process?

◊ How should individuals in the organization relate to a hierarchically driven planning process? What expectations might you have for them?

◊ Among the formal approaches to planning noted in the literature and available through consultants, which ones will best accommodate the conclusions you reached above?

◊ How is team-based problem solving accommodated if you currently have an achievement-oriented compensation system developed from individual contracts?

◊ Is team accountability necessarily measured by the same metric as individual accountability, and what needs to be added so that the team has synergy?

Or, for example, in an individual DNA–based organization,

◊ How are external stakeholders taken into account and rewarded when the system is loosely woven and employees' needs require sustained attention and accommodation?

◊ Does this suggest that a new role or portfolio needs to be added?

SUMMARY

The process of alignment creates new problems to solve and puzzles to ponder. The practices within each DNA type offer challenges and raise possibilities for potential solutions or directions that will accommodate the logic, the DNA, of the organization. The interventions and actions required should be based on the negotiation of the space in-between practices as leaders and organizational members create and maintain the appropriate tactical harmony and face the challenges of new issues and realities.

The Clash of DNA

When two organizations come together for the purpose of a merger or other alliance, they stand a strong chance of encountering a clash of differing DNA types. In some instances this clash may be resolved. It is more probable, however, that the organizational differences will cause great strain and potentially even lead to a failure.

In this chapter we examine the organizational adjustments required to accommodate a variety of situations involving a clash of DNA types: a change in leadership, a merger or acquisition, development of consortia or partnerships, organizational decline, and organizational development from one stage to another. Scenarios are presented for each situation, in which the outcomes for the organization may have been less than ideal. Using what you know about organizational DNA, you are challenged to develop an alternative resolution of each issue.

Our observations on these scenarios are provided at the end of the chapter. These observations are not designed to be fully developed answers to the questions posed, but rather are further reflections on each scenario. Also keep in mind that the scenarios included represent a small sampling of the range of elements requiring adjustment when organizations engage the issues presented below.

CHANGE IN LEADERSHIP

A change in leadership can occur at the organizational level, at a department or division level, or even at the work unit level. What happens if the new leadership has a different DNA type than what has been functioning in that setting? Can the organization transform to align with the new leaders' DNA or do the new leaders have to change their mode of operating. Does this create stress for the organization or for the manager?

Leadership Scenario 1 (L1): From Individual to Conceptual

Organization A, a thirty-year-old process-oriented manufacturing company, was founded by a husband-and-wife team. They led the firm based on their individual knowledge of the process, allowing each manager to work however he or she saw fit. There were few rules or regulations. It was expected that people would perform, and if they did not, they were dismissed.

The founders were nearing retirement age. Their son became president of the company. He decided to run the company based on the idea of everyone working toward best serving the customer. Whenever any issue came up, the first question to be asked was, "Is this what my customer would expect?"

The organizational leadership was transitioning from individual DNA to conceptual DNA. What issues would the leaders have to face in making this transition?

(For our observations, see L1, page 120)

Leadership Scenario 2 (L2): From Individual to Factual

A public utility was very stable, with an organizational culture that was much like a family. The workers had specialized skills and generally worked alone. The work got done, and the public was served, but there were few deadlines set, and pressure was rarely applied if targets were missed. Employees had a commitment to the public, but once the required work was done they often did not do anything else. People could be found reading newspapers at their desks until the next project was placed in front of them.

A new executive director was hired. Her style was very detail and fact oriented. She managed by setting goals and meeting face-to-face with each of her managers on a weekly or bi-weekly basis. She required that each employee set goals and that performance toward these goals be reported on regularly.

As she surveyed the organization, she realized that for the most part the work was done in a professional manner. She felt, however, that one section that was more involved in operations could be better managed by a firm that specialized in that area. She negotiated to outsource the work, with the remaining professionals in that section overseeing the contract.

The employees in the organization did not respond well to this transition. Outsourcing their former co-workers' work was viewed as spilling the lifeblood of the organization. Morale plummeted; complaints soared.

Bit by bit, the enterprise was reorganized to align with the executive's perspective. Departmental alliances were altered and the performance review process was amended. Concurrently, top-level managers were replaced, and some managers and other professionals chose to leave. Five years later the organization had substantially completed a transition from an individual DNA–based organization to a factual DNA–based one.

> Using your knowledge of organizational DNA, how might
> you have handled the situation?
>
> *(For our observations, see L2, page 121)*

MERGERS AND ACQUISITIONS

Unique issues arise when two organizations of different DNA types
come together either through a merger or an acquisition. How do
the two types come together? Can the leaders of both organizations
survive?

Merger and Acquisition Scenario 1 (MA1):
Merging Contextual and Factual

Two union-based building contractor companies, both long established in a medium-sized community, were merging to form one company. Company A placed a strong value on functioning like a family—
people cared for one another, and many of its employees were in fact
related. When a challenge arose they rallied around to meet the challenge. Almost everyone attended company picnics and Christmas
parties—and brought their families along. Labor and management
respected one another.

At company B people came in and did their job, and they did it well.
On the whole, employees did not spend much time together after
work. Work was work, and family was family. There was a strong belief
by management that they were in control and that union employees
should do as they were told.

For a variety of reasons, the two company presidents decided to
merge their organizations. The president from company B would be
chief executive officer; the president from company A, chief operating
officer. After two years and the apparent absorption of the family-

oriented, contextual DNA–based company by the factual DNA–based company, the COO decided to retire early.

> Given what you know about organizational DNA, how might this situation have been handled differently?
>
> *(For our observations, see MA1, page 121)*

Merger and Acquisition Scenario 2 (MA2): Factual Acquiring Conceptual

A multinational German-based manufacturer acquired a U.S. firm that made the same product. The U.S. firm, while strongly engineering focused, was based on the concept that, above all else, the product should fit the needs of the customer. When designing new products, customers were brought in to help with design.

The German firm was run by engineers who knew their product and took pride in their expertise. They considered customer issues but relied more heavily on their abilities as professional engineers. The differences of opinion led to internal squabbling and delays in design and production. Sales of the product plummeted in the U.S. Many members of the U.S.-based management were let go.

> Could these events have been anticipated?
>
> *(For our observations, see MA2, page 121)*

CONSORTIA AND PARTNERSHIPS

There are many instances where forming a consortium or partnership is a better strategy for an organization than to merge formally. Here also there may be a conflict between the DNA types of the organizations involved.

Consortia and Partnerships Scenario 1 (CP1): Partnering of Contextual and Conceptual

Two colleges, a contextual DNA–based organization (college A) and a conceptual DNA–based organization (college B), were in an open-ended collaborative relationship. They each hoped to share resources in their respective parts of the country or resources owned by them that could be of value to the other. For example, college A shipped biological materials for students to study, and college B sent slides of important artworks for student use. However, while contextual college A could share its resources, conceptual college B, in spite of its commitment to the relationship, dominated the interactions due to its idea-based identity and thus intruded on the focus and legitimacy of college A. Individuals from college A were required to engage in long visits to college B. Upon returning home, they would be considered traitors by their colleagues who had "remained in their place."

There were additional differences between these systems, in terms of history, constituencies, and financial soundness, which made a long-term relationship an unreachable goal. What made this an especially difficult situation was that it was the differences that had led to the relationship in the first place. Yet, the two parties were surprised when they realized the power of the differences in forestalling continuing interactions.

> Given that sharing each other's different strengths is often a reason for partnering, how might this pattern be engaged to work effectively among organizations of different types?
>
> *(For our observations, see CP1, page 122)*

Consortia and Partnerships Scenario 2 (CP2): Partnering of Factual and Contextual

Organizations generally join as partners either to gain resources or to solve problems, or both. Yet, these practices are based on different needs. For an organization to partner around resources, its partner must not be in competition for the same things. This suggests that differences around resource interests are critical for positive relationship development. Problem solving is an entirely different matter, in that similarities provide the grounds for understanding mutual needs and potentially genuine communication around issues.

> In terms of these two partnering goals, how would a factual DNA–based organization and a contextual DNA–based organization decide on how to develop interaction so that they could both gain from the relationship and solve mutual issues?
>
> *(For our observations, see CP2, page 122)*

STAGE-TO-STAGE DEVELOPMENT/MATURATION

The literature on organizational life-cycle evolution, including the difficult transitions between stages, does not take into account that organizations have basic differences in terms of DNA and other considerations. This makes it exceedingly difficult to begin to understand the kinds of changes that take place and the nature of the transitions. While more research on this subject is required, we pose the following scenario for review.

Development/Maturation Scenario 1 (DM1):
Maturing Individual

It can be assumed that development, or maturation in general, is informed by a factual-oriented logic. The clash here occurs when ideas are brought from an individual DNA–generated development/maturation model to another kind of system where they may not fit. It is necessary to begin thinking in alternative terms. This is just what you would need to do when confronted with an organizational issue for which there is no good set of alternative observations.

Currently, regardless of DNA type, we know that the suggested movement is always toward greater formalization and stability, followed by some splitting apart into departments or divisions, a process known as differentiation. This predictably leads to the need for integration and, then again, an ability to see things in a fresh way.

> What are the transitional challenges experienced by organizations having different DNA types?
>
> *(For our observations, see DM1, page 122)*

ORGANIZATIONAL DECLINE

The issue of organizational decline, whether evidenced in the demise of "dot-coms" or in retrenchments, sports a massive literature (see Cameron et al. 1988 for a useful collection). It identifies decline with an organization's failure to make effective transitions between life stages; its failure to deal effectively with the market and its particular niche, such as the failure to read environmental changes; or its suffering a lack of confidence due to, say, an ethical challenge. As well, the literature focuses on the consequences of such decline for individuals as well as the larger system (often increased rigidification) and on approaches for managing the decline, say, through the invitation to be open to solutions at variance with current practices. Here, as earlier, from the accounts and research available it is not possible to know the kinds of organizations—in terms of our DNA types—that are associated with the potential consequences.

The following examples are provided to suggest some possibilities from among many potential scenarios that might involve the clash of DNA types. Once again, the clash is not between or among organizations; rather it is around the ideas brought into the experience from potentially incompatible exemplars.

Organizational Decline Scenario 1 (OD1): Declining Contextual

An organization based on strong relationships was faced with an economic downturn that would require a six-week layoff of approximately one-third of the company's employees. The company had never done a layoff before.

Seniority had never been used as a delineator and was not viewed as appropriate since all employees were valued equally. After much discussion, it was decided that a rotating layoff scheme would be used. For the first two weeks one-third of the employees would be out of work; another one-third would take the second two weeks; the remainder would take the last two weeks.

A problem arose when, after the first group took their layoff, the company received an unexpected order and the second two groups did not have to be laid off at all. A couple of years later, when the company experienced another economic downturn, the employees suggested that rather than a layoff, they should all take a cut in pay for the duration of the downturn.

> Might there have been another way to achieve the same goal, while honoring the integrity of the organization?
>
> *(For our observations, see OD1, page 123)*

Organizational Decline Scenario 2 (OD2):
New Leadership in a Nonprofit

A nonprofit organization was founded to support a particular commitment to the development of an ideal society, through the sponsorship of books, conferences, and a retreat for scholars whose ideas were compatible with the founding vision. As is often the case for conceptual-based, socially conscious organizations, as the political environment changed, the visionaries in the organization got older and either moved on or were unable to carry on as active managers.

The board members were aware that the original vision could not be sustained without an infusion of resources and that new resources would likely be attached to interests that would test and put at risk the founding ideas. Yet, they were realists who recognized the changing political and social climate in the country. They hired an entrepreneurial CEO who was experienced in community-based nonprofits with the challenge to partner with other parties and organizations that would bring in needed resources.

> What would you have the new CEO do to remedy the absence of a supportive environment?
>
> *(For our observations, see OD2, page 123)*

OBSERVATIONS ON
ORGANIZATIONAL SCENARIOS

L1: Many entrepreneurial organizations have an individual DNA type that reflects the founder's drive to succeed. When a new leader is introduced there is often resistance to change. "But this is not the way we have always done it" can be heard as new approaches are tried. As this particular organization transitioned to a second generation, the new president introduced his direction by talking directly to employees. Whenever a problem came up, rather than solve it he asked, "How does this affect our customers?" Gradually employees began to understand and started to ask themselves the question rather than going to the president for assistance.

L2: Had we been in this situation, we might have tried to resolve the issues from within rather than outsourcing a major portion of the organization. It is likely that the transition would have gone much more smoothly. To make this work, however, it is also likely that some major changes in leadership and organizational practices would have been necessary. In this case, however, the new CEO was chosen because her style was so different and there was a perception that a major overhaul was in order. The process of gradually transitioning to the fact-based internal work systems as well as the reinforcement of face-to-face, data-oriented leadership helped to move the organization to reflect the new DNA. It is important to note, however, that the process took five years and the replacement of many of those in leadership positions.

MA1: Often in mergers and acquisitions only the factual business details are attended to. A clear division of responsibility should be agreed to in advance with a common understanding of the relationship by employees. Here the factual-based CEO could have taken responsibility for long-term strategy while the contextual-based COO could have taken responsibility for labor/management relations and the monitoring of day-to-day management of projects. This might have kept the company focused while at the same time allowing for the development of relationships.

MA2: A factual DNA–based organization always has great comparative legitimacy in difficult times, since it is the bottom line that is generally at issue, and this type of system speaks the language stockholders want to hear. To survive as a merged organization with equal rights, the conceptual system must anticipate this outcome and work to counteract it. This can be done by giving the merged system more time to demonstrate the value of synergy—not evaluating it too early—and to ensure that each partner contributes necessary components for success.

CP1: There is a need to calibrate the interactions such that the ideological or conceptual focus of one party does not provide the definition and legitimacy of its partner. At the same time, it has to be recognized that the legitimacy of the conceptual partner has value for the contextual organization outside its own setting. The veneer of the former was dismissed internally by the latter but celebrated externally to provide legitimacy with certain important stakeholders. Recognizing the strategic value of the relationship, and recognizing the skewed dynamic (and offering differential rewards), might have enhanced the viability of the joint enterprise.

CP2: Distributing or allocating rewards and solving problems are evident in a variety of social negotiations, primarily in labor negotiations, but also in international diplomacy. Examinations of practices here would provide exemplars in the joint achievement of these two outcomes—the effective division of resources and the solving of problems—as they demand alternative grounds for action. The issue is how to combine competition and cooperation in a way that intertwines them so that success in one sector fuels success in the other.

DM1: Here we need to look at alternative systems to appreciate their developmental trajectory. Social forces are such that the movement is usually considered in relation to a factual DNA-based system since organizations often develop by reacting to external dynamics in the marketplace, as opposed to simply moving toward greater formality.

Organizations do not need to "grow up" as a measure of their success. They may want to remain effective according to the original formula, making only those changes that would allow their continuance. This means that parties need to maintain the early values and associated risks, which, while difficult as they experience change, is not impossible. Volunteer and community-based organizations are good exemplars. A chamber music society may have the same basic challenges year after year, and the same needs, though incremental changes might be accommodated by existing mechanisms. There may or may not be significant developmental necessities.

OD1: In this case, through experimentation, the organization reached an acceptable resolution. The first solution was felt to be unfair because two-thirds of the employees did not share in the layoff. In the second round, all shared equally in the decline with every employee receiving a reduced paycheck. The relationship-based context was protected.

OD2: The challenge is in not becoming a factual DNA–based organization by using the old rhetoric to support a hidden but different reality. It is not uncommon for conceptual DNA–based organizations to transform type when seeking greater stability. Of course, this alienates those committed to the founding ideas and replaces them with those who are associated with interests that will abandon them. The challenge is to reinvent the organization by inviting fresh foundational thinking that could provide the energy for a necessary retransformation as a conceptual DNA–based organization.

CONCLUSION

This book focuses on organizational character and management practices. We have used these materials with others who work with and in organizations, assisting them in attaining alignment between their practices and their DNA. As it turns out, supporting and enhancing the alignment of systems is not only a value-constituted issue, it is also related to system effectiveness. Achieving organizational and individual integrity or alignment is the foundation for a holistic approach that is both rewarding and motivating. It supports growth and development that feel natural in the organization and is not a fabrication related to processes that "just don't fit."

We suggest that you describe and write down your observations of organizational practices. Where are the clues for identifying the most prevalent type of DNA? At this point you should be able to examine various organizational practices, as described in our charts and examples, and decide which of the four DNA types seems most relevant and appropriate to your experience. Once you can see management practices and your organizational components in terms of their interacting complexities, you will be able to identify areas that might be considered for deliberate change so as to develop the alignment that will bring integrity into your system.

We ask that you look at the interfaces between the various systems—individual and organizational, personal and work related. Identities are often the consequence of the press of different systems on each other: as we work together, we and our settings define each other. Observers need to be in a position to see these mutual influences and to manage them as they evolve toward greater or lesser equilibrium, which in their various stabilizations have different value for us and our organizations.

Around these systems, we can situate ourselves close up, at a distance, or on the boundary between them. We can observe at full light or at dusk and see different things. We recommend that you look at patterns across the organization as various systems influence others and, perhaps under different conditions, are influenced by others.

As with our own work, we suggest that each approach to gathering data includes in its own way the alternatives in the range. We are all engineers, philosophers, social scientists, and boundary agents—but in different ways. We can all focus on facts, concepts, contexts, and individuals, and it is up to each of us to discover how this will work for our own situation as we consider their relationships.

From a factual base, we can assess the goals that are operative and, for example, be aware of data on environmental factors and human resources. From a conceptual base, we can get to know the sources of meaningful ideas and how they are promoted and used. From a contextual base, we can understand how the various DNA types interact with each other. And, from an individual base, we can understand how the relationships among different kinds of systems affect human goals.

Think as well about how others operate from their own bases. This will allow you to be more effective as you relate to other individuals and units in your organization whose DNA perspective is different from your own. When you are effectively learning from your base DNA and when you can understand how others operate, beyond building more effective organizations, you will also become a life-long learner and experience greater holism and joy in your life.

Empowerment Resources

E ach of the four organizational examples in this book chose a different path to employee empowerment. For Springfield Remanufacturing Corporation (SRC) it was putting in place a routinized structure of meetings focused on the profit-and-loss statement and teaching all employees about the bottom line. At Johnsonville Sausage the path was centered on the unifying concept of each employee becoming responsible for his or her own performance. Leadership sets a general direction for the company, but, beyond that, employees have sizable latitude. At YSI a system of interlocking teams was established that allowed people to work together toward mutually agreed-on goals. At Wainwright Industries employees may choose their activities as long as they positively contribute toward their five strategic indicators.

Each approach to empowerment reflects the respective organization's DNA. If factual DNA–based SRC had attempted to use a contextual, team-based approach to empowerment, or if conceptual DNA–based Johnsonville Sausage had tried to use a factual approach, they both likely would have failed.

Your mission, then, is to determine your organization's DNA and then assess the resources available—including consultants, workshops, and written materials such as those cited below—based upon DNA alignment.

RESOURCES

We start with empowerment resources from our exemplar organizations. The CEOs of two of these companies have written best-selling business books on empowerment. Springfield CEO Jack Stack's *Great Game of Business* (1992) nicely outlines his factual DNA-based approach. Johnsonville's Ralph Stayer co-authored *Flight of the Buffalo* (Belasco and Stayer 1993), identifying how to unify behind an organizational concept. SRC, Johnsonville Sausage, and Wainwright Industries have offered workshops on how to implement what they have been doing successfully in terms of their own DNA. Wainwright Industries' video *Sincere Trust and Belief in People* (1997) details their management/employee philosophy.

Beyond these resources so obviously reinforcing the organizational DNA of the companies presenting them, there are several other valuable books available. *Empowerment in Organizations* (Vogt and Murrell 1990) and *The Open-Book Experience* (Case 1998) offer a relatively straightforward recipe appropriate for factual DNA-based organizations.

McLagan and Nel (1997) exemplify conceptual DNA with a vivid description of organizations empowering employees by centering on the concepts of governance and participation. For contextual DNA a team-oriented approach is advocated by Katzenbach and Smith (1993) as well as by Ray and Bronstein (1995). Margaret Wheatley (1992) exemplifies individual DNA through a chaotic networked system she defines as "self-organizing work systems."

Organizational Learning Resources

The topics of organizational learning, learning organizations, and knowledge management are relatively recent additions to the interventionist's repertoire. Yet, such orientations have actually been around a long time, occurring naturally in the everyday actions of individuals, groups or teams, and the organization as a whole, either minus the identifying labels or with different labels.

Unlike today's organizational learning material, older work was committed to providing balance (Farber 2000) to the extant views of organizational functioning. This was accomplished by looking at the dysfunctions of organizational practices supported by organizational theories (Thompson 1961), the use of satire (Stroup 1966), repositioning exemplary practices (Barnard 1938), and through research (Blau 1973). As well, there were attempts to correct the dysfunctions of organizations in their variety (Etzioni 1961, Katz and Kahn 1966) through organizational development, such as by opening up (McCall 1979) and rethinking managerial actions (Argyris 1992).

Our view of organizations today using "DNA logic" suggests two directions regarding organizational learning in the contemporary environment: organizations can be seen as evolving either within similarly understood contexts or in environments in which multiple logics are also in use. There are ways of thinking about organizational learning, then, that accommodate both versions.

ORGANIZATIONAL LEARNING BY DNA TYPE

The scope of this book is such that we are not able to fully present, describe, or evaluate all the various tools and approaches that are available, as located under the DNA headings we provide, as they relate to learning or knowledge management activities. We have to be satisfied with identifying, as exemplars, approaches and strategies that you can engage such that the tools you employ effectively relate to the DNA logic of your organization.

Factual DNA–Based Learning

How does a fact- or data-based organization learn? Well, to put it both simply and accurately, with facts and data—and there is no lack of appropriate tools. One of the best known is Kaplan and Norton's *The Balanced Scorecard* (1996), used initially for firms and often reinvented for other organizational settings. Data regarding objectives, measures, targets, and initiatives relate to internal business processes, the customer, the financial picture, and learning and growth. Subsequent measures relating to each perspective are used for strategic direction setting and accomplishment.

As well, Gormley and Weimer (1999) developed "organizational report cards" to monitor performance, and serve accountability, by looking at inputs, processes, and outcomes in relation to the review of audiences who they identify as consumers, policymakers, and service providers (94) to include their ability to interpret the information. Their book discusses numerous issues including "blending quantitative and qualitative information into ratings" (71), "distilling expert judgment into algorithms" (73), and "incorporating information from direct observation" (74).

There are also additional metric-oriented treatments such as Sveiby's (2000) "Measuring Intangibles and Intellectual Capital," monitoring such indicators as those related to growth, renewal, efficiency, and stability/risk. Bassi and Van Buren (2000), in a section titled "What Isn't Measured Isn't (Well) Managed," focus on indicators such as employee commitment and the percentage of the workforce involved in innovation.

While the authors of these texts provide data around their measurement devices, scholars unaffiliated with an intervention do research and use methodologies that support learning in a factual DNA-based organization. Whether based on simulations or data from actual settings, research may focus on questions that are relevant to an intervention such as the learning situation of either hierarchies or teams when new persons with different experience join them to work on different kinds of tasks (Carley 1992).

Conceptual DNA–Based Learning

Organizational learning in this DNA dimension often takes the form of executing learning tasks related to directions from major propositions. Often related to systems theory or other purportedly generalizable knowledge claims, organizational learning is here presented as having universal value. The dissemination of knowledge takes place from a central or more informed location.

The centerpiece of such work is *The Fifth Discipline* (Senge 1990). Senge states that "five new component technologies are gradually converging to innovate learning organizations" (6), including systems thinking, personal mastery, mental models, building of shared vision, and team learning. Senge quite obviously speaks to substantial, large, directive-oriented ideas that are congruent with conceptual DNA-based organizations.

Ives, Torrey, and Gordon (2000) tackle the sharing of knowledge, identifying several dissemination locations and methods.

> Knowledge sharing is best supported by a two-part organizational structure with professional dedicated knowledge management staff who own the knowledge processes, templates and technologies, and knowledge sponsors, integrators, and developers from the business units who own the knowledge content.... The professional knowledge management staff can guide and support employees through the act of knowledge sharing. (103)

In *Firms As Knowledge Brokers* Hargadon (1998) details the functions of these "brokers" as they share their approaches, say, in transferring knowledge. The author notes four key tactics whereby organizations explore new territories, learn something about everything, find hidden connections, and "make the damn thing work" (225–26).

On a more common level, "benchmarking" qualifies as a learning approach that relies on ideas seen as exemplars, or as models for others, which is congruent with the idea-based organizational DNA.

Contextual DNA–Based Learning

It could be argued that in a generic sense all organizational learning is contextual. Similarly, organizational development engages a variety of organizational contexts such as teams in terms of communication skills and the organization as a whole in such areas as strategic planning. It would seem that these would qualify as learning events. While learning takes place, there are clearly foci to learning that relate to this DNA dimension that begin by asking about the logic of knowledge either needed in, or relevant to, organizations. That is, there appears to be greater attention to fundamentals and somewhat less attention to traditional interventions whose foundations have been fairly well established.

A fundamental view for a contextual treatment is provided by Brown and Duguid's (1991) discussion in "Organizational Learning and Communities of Practice." They agree with Lave and Wenger

(1991) that learning is related to the conditions of learning as one becomes a community member, as individuals become insiders (69). They argue the value of emergent communities enacting interpretations of the environment and focus on organizations as "communities-of-communities."

> Within an organization perceived as a collective of communities, not simply of individuals, in which enacting experiments are legitimate, separate community perspectives can be amplified by interchanges among communities. Out of this friction can come the sort of improvisational sparks necessary for igniting organizational innovation. (77–78)

Huber (1991) focuses on the breadth of knowledge an organization needs, including vicarious knowing, the distribution and interpretation of information, and organizational unlearning, among other topics, all with a contextual grounding.

Van der Heijden and Eden (1998) examine learning in relation to strategic planning, exploring the relation between individual, group, and organizational understandings. They bring ways of understanding the environment "relevant to developing an understanding of sense-making and shared meaning as it relates to organizational learning" (65).

Moving from learning's use to its management in organizations, Reinhardt (2000) considers different learning levels, modes, types, and phases, and their management. In addition to implementation stages, such as preparation and presentation, he includes barriers that relate to failures such as secrecy, which denies the availability of information to organizational participants (197).

And, we should recognize also that the learning context is not only internal to the organization but also relates to external contingencies. Teece's (1998) paper on the market and information flows associated with the flow of goods and services (59) relates to his treatment of competitive advantage, concluding with a theory of the firm—"its ability to create, transfer, assemble, integrate, and exploit knowledge assets" (75).

All of these writers put the context as location, and embed their propositions and metrics into or with the organization rather than shape to its measurements or externally based ideas.

Individual DNA–Based Learning

While there is less material relevant to learning organizations in this dimension than to the others, in our judgment Peter Vaill speaks forcibly and intelligently to the individual focus, as reflected by the title of his book *Learning As a Way of Being* (1996). Arguing that we are in "permanent white water," he sees learning as a response and defines it as "changes a person makes in himself or herself that increase the know-why and/or the know-what and/or the know-how the person possesses with respect to a given subject" (21).

He sees the need for learning that is self-directed, creative, expressive, continual, on line, and reflexive—and a need for these foci to be interwoven (56–57). His treatment centers on the interweaving of these foci, with his orientation on leadership, labeled "leaderly learning," reflecting challenges having similar dimensions (133). For example, in addressing "feeling leaderly learning" he argues,

> Facts do not speak for themselves, for if they did, humans would find it easy to agree. Meanings, implications, significances, and portents are *wrested* from the flow of events, wrested by men and women who have a felt stake in how things are unfolding. (141)

He deals with the other DNA dimensions through his attention on technical facts and his marvelous work on "purposing," which has to do with "establishing a 'mission' and a 'vision'" (146). He notes that "a leader with relational knowledge and skill makes purposes and technical facts and realities meaningful to all the various stakeholders he or she encounters" (146). Interestingly, although he addresses the other dimensions, he clearly makes the individual the primary dimension under which the others lie.

There are additional treatments that highlight the individual DNA-based dimension. Work on dialogues devoted to learning (Hodgson 1997); co-operative inquiry and self-reflection (Marshall and Reason 1997); incidental and informal learning (Marsick and Watkins 1997); coaching, group or team processes, and individuals' cognitive/causal mapping (Eden and Ackermann 1998), which when analyzed blends into the ideational dimension, are but some of the approaches for individual learning in organizations.

INTEGRATED DNA LEARNING MODELS

While there are approaches to organizational learning that can be located in each of the four DNA types, there are numerous models that accommodate all of them either in some sequence or as reflecting alternatives within a particular author's grounding principles. Here we have models or delineations of organizational learning that can be considered complete in the sense that each one embodies all four dimensions. Typically, they are each presented in texts that include case examples such that the pattern or rhythm associated with each approach can be appreciated both experientially and logically.

There has been little research regarding how this learning approach—that is, one based on a comprehensive model or a more focused one—relates to different outcomes on the basis of any pattern of ideas such as its long- or short-term value, efficiency or effectiveness for the individual or organization, the resilience of individuals or communities, strategic positioning, or any number of possibilities. So, we would especially urge those who use the various ideas and models to be alert to the differentiated value of these learning models and approaches and to share them with colleagues.

In terms of these comprehensive models, the various components do, in fact, have no choice but to redefine the organizational space in terms of the logical variety evident in the models. This leads to alternative possible application approaches. One approach would be to first define the organizational type and craft the learning activities to the dominant system in the same way we embedded alternative definitions of practices. That is, we might take our four-DNA-type model and see how it relates to the embeddedness of the various logics under a dominant type.

While the full cycles of learning activities have relevance for specific systems, often the individuals who are involved in the various parts of a learning cycle differ, as the pattern evolves and as the different outcomes are developed. So, in this approach it would make sense to consider the organization as differentiated into subsystems that would relate more effectively to the multiple logics in the model.

Models Reflecting a Primary Approach

Sparrow's (1998) model is comprehensive but located in the individual DNA–based logic. He focuses on a variety of thought processes, such as autistic thinking, or the free-flowing and intuitive sense that individuals have about things; mood, which is about how material is processed; and reasoning, which is differentiated in terms of a variety of parameters. We account for more or less of something, separate things, locate them differently. He notes that location thinking has different facets regarding how things fit together—causal thinking, systems thinking, and plurality seeking, that is, for the latter, recognizing a wider cultural and historical context of interpretation. He deals with forms of thought and continues with interesting and complex representations of knowledge. Here it could be argued that the variety of logics is present as embedded under the individual cognitive approach.

As well, Baumard (1999) differentiates knowledge as explicit/tacit and individual/collective in its possibilities that lead to four different modalities that he identifies with a large number of scholars' works on knowledge. Collective/explicit relates to objectified knowledge;

individual/explicit to conscious knowledge; collective/tacit to collective knowledge; and individual/tacit to learning without awareness. He "loops through" these knowing modes, suggesting relationships among them, which he identifies as assimilation, articulation, socialization, and implicit learning through these transitions and conversions. In this framework, the dominant organizing notion is "ideas," which also have parameters that reflect the various DNA dimensions in this book. These are articulated into such themes as dealing with the unexpressed, elusive know-how, and moving from the tacit to the explicit, where he develops a typology reflecting categories of knowledge, interestingly posited as *techne* (capability and task accomplishment), *episteme* (abstract generalization), *pronesis* (practical and social wisdom), and *metis* (conjectural intelligence).

He also compares them on thirteen attributes, such as their structure and method (55), and relates them to the variables in his original model. He notes these four types of knowledge to be inseparable and looks at various strategies regarding their interaction. Coming across this typology in the process of examining the learning literature is just what happens to us as authors as we continually find serendipitous support for the basic model explicated in this book.

In another work that looks at learning style, experts/continuous improvers, copiers/benchmarkers, experimenters/innovators, and competent workers/skill acquirers are related by Yeung et al. (1999) to different business cultures (hierarchy, market, adhocracy, and clan) and organizational performance in terms of competitiveness, innovativeness, and new product introduction. Arguably, this model privileges four modes of learning in a contextual frame.

Models Reflecting a Cycle of Events

There are models that suggest a cycle of events. Often connected with examples from a single organization tracing projects over the long term or examining organizational learning from the experiences of numerous firms that provide exemplars of a model's validity, this is a very exciting literature that suggests for us the most difficulty in attending to organizational logics. That is, as noted earlier, each parameter of the full model suggests alternative organizational logic.

Nonaka and Takeuchi (1995) suggest that the direction for organizational learning is from tacit knowing to creating concepts to justifying concepts to building an archetype and then to cross-leveling knowledge, or inter- and intraorganizational extension. That is, we start with individual logic, move to conceptual, then factual, then contextual, and finally to cross-leveling of knowledge, which is the spiraling process that "triggers a new cycle of knowledge creation, expanding horizontally and vertically across the organization" (88). Their model is richer than what is presented above, but the intent here is to suggest the primary presence of all four logics.

Nonaka and Takeuchi also note the use of "middle-up-down management," by which they mean the spiral conversion of knowledge through middle managers who lead teams and task forces. It is their engagement as bridges that supports the power of this work in relation to our multiple logics of action as they deal most effectively in managing boundaries and communicating across contexts (129–30).

Shukla (1997) moves from discovered knowledge (which is personal, tacit, creative) to codified knowledge (which is explicit, tangible, proprietary) to migratory knowledge (which is mobile and propagates) to invisible knowledge (which is absorbed, embedded). So then, we start with individual DNA logic, move to factual, then contextual, and finally conceptual. Nonaka and Takeuchi, and Shukla, both begin with the individual frame but then differ considerably.

Whether you use a specialized approach to organizational learning that relates to one of the logical DNA types—employing it as the primary idea or foundation and embedding the others within it—or a generic model that also contains the four DNA logics in its architecture, attention needs to be placed on the whole system for it to prosper.

Bibliography

Adelman, H. 1973. *The holiversity: A perspective on the Wright report.* Toronto: New Press.

Adler, P. S., and B. Borys. 1996. Two types of bureaucracy: Enabling and coercive. *Administrative Science Quarterly* 41:61–89.

Anderson, C. W. 1993. Prescribing the life of the mind: An essay on the purpose of the university, the aims of liberal education, the competence of citizens, and the cultivation of practical reason. Madison, WI: University of Wisconsin Press.

Argyris, C. 1992. *On organizational learning.* Cambridge, MA: Blackwell.

Barnard, C. I. 1938. *The functions of the executive.* Cambridge, MA: Harvard University Press.

Bassi, L. J., and M. E. Van Buren. 2000. New measures for a new era. In *Knowledge management: Classic and contemporary works.* Ed. D. Morey et al. Cambridge, MA: MIT Press, 355–73.

Baumard, P. 1999. *Tacit knowledge in organizations.* London: Sage.

Belasco, J., and R. Stayer. 1993. *Flight of the buffalo.* New York: Warner Books.

Blau, P. M. 1973. *The organization of academic work.* New York: Wiley.

Brown, J. S., and P. Duguid. 1991. Organizational learning and communities-of-practice. *Organization Science* 2(1).

Cameron, K. S., et al., eds. 1988. *Readings in organizational decline: Frameworks, research, and prescriptions.* Cambridge, MA: Ballinger.

Carley, K. 1992. Organizational learning and personnel turnover. *Organization Science* 3(1).

Case, J. 1993. A company of business people. *Inc. Magazine* (April): 79–82.

_____. 1998. *The open-book experience.* New York: Addison-Wesley.

Collins, H., and M. Kusch. 1998. *The shape of actions: What humans and machines can do.* Cambridge, MA: MIT Press.

Detienne, M. 1996. *The masters of truth in archaic Greece.* New York: Zone.

Eden, C., and F. Ackermann. 1998. Analyzing and comparing idiographic causal maps. In *Managerial and organizational cognition: Theory, methods and research.* Ed. C. Eden and J. C. Spender. London: Sage.

Etzioni, A. 1961. *A comparative analysis of complex organizations: On power, involvement, and their correlates.* New York: Free Press.

Farber, P. L. 2000. *Finding order in nature: The naturalist tradition from Linnaeus to E. O. Wilson.* Baltimore: Johns Hopkins Press.

Fisher, D., and W. R. Torbert. 1995. *Personal and organizational transformations: The true challenge of continual quality improvement.* London: McGraw-Hill.

Fuchs, S. 1992. *The professional quest for truth: A social theory of science and knowledge.* Albany, NY: SUNY Press.

Gormley, W. T., and D. L. Weimer. 1999. *Organizational report cards.* Cambridge, MA: Harvard University Press.

Hargadon, A. B. 1998. Firms as knowledge brokers: Lessons in pursuing continuous innovation. *California Management Review* (Special issue on knowledge and the firm) 40(3):209–27.

Hassard, J., and M. Parker. 1993. *Postmodernism and organizations.* Thousand Oaks, CA: Sage.

Hodgson, V. 1997. New technology and learning: Accepting the challenge. In *Management learning: Integrating perspectives in theory and practice.* Ed. J. Burgoyne and M. Reynolds. London: Sage, 215–22.

Honold, L. K. 1998. Johnsonville Sausage: A case study of a learning organization. Learning Company Conference, Warwick, England.

_____. 1999. An empowered organization: A consideration of professional and theoretical alternatives. Ph.D. diss., The Fielding Institute, Santa Barbara, CA.

Huber, G. P. 1991. Organizational learning: The contributing processes and the literatures. *Organization Science* 2(1).

Ives, W., et al. 2000. Knowledge sharing is a human behavior. In *Knowledge management: Classic and contemporary works*. Ed. D. Morey et al. Cambridge, MA: MIT Press.

Kaplan, R. S., and D. P. Norton. 1996. *The balanced scorecard: Translating strategy into action*. Boston: Harvard Business School Press.

Katz, D., and R. L. Kahn. 1966. *The social psychology of organization*. New York: Wiley.

Katzenbach, J. R., and D. Smith. 1993. *The wisdom of teams: Creating the high-performance organization*. Boston: Harvard Business School Press.

Keeley, M. 1988. *A social-contract theory of organizations*. Notre Dame, IN: University of Notre Dame Press.

Kerr, S. 1975. On the folly of rewarding A, while hoping for B. *Academy of Management Journal* 18(4):769–83.

Klein, J. A. 1994. The paradox of quality management: Commitment, ownership, and control. In *The post-bureaucratic organization: New perspectives on organizational change*. Ed. C. Hechscher and A. Donnellon. Thousand Oaks, CA: Sage, 178–94.

Kostera, M., and A. Kozminski. 2001. Four theatres: Moral discourses in Polish management. *Management Learning* 32(3):321–43.

Lave, J., and E. Wenger. 1991. *Situated learning: Legitimate peripheral participation*. New York: Cambridge University Press.

Levin, D. M. 1989. *The listening self: Personal growth, social change and the closure of metaphysics*. London: Routledge.

Marshall, J., and P. Reason. 1997. Collaborative and self-reflective forms of inquiry in management research. In *Management learning: Integrating perspectives in theory and practice*. Ed. J. Burgoyne and M. Reynolds. London: Sage, 226–42.

Marsick, V. J., and K. E. Watkins. 1997. Lessons from informal and incidental learning. In *Management learning: Integrating perspectives in theory and practice*. Ed. J. Burgoyne and M. Reynolds. London: Sage, 295–311.

McCall, M. 1979. Conjecturing about creative leaders. *Journal of Creative Behavior* 14(4):225–34.

McGregor, D. 1960. *The human side of enterprise*. New York: McGraw-Hill.

McKeon, R. 1994. *On knowing: The natural sciences.* Chicago: University of Chicago Press.

McLagan, P., and C. Nel. 1997. *The age of participation: New governance for the workplace and the world.* San Francisco: Berrett-Koehler.

Nonaka, I., and H. Takeuchi. 1995. *The knowledge-creating company: How Japanese companies create the dynamics of innovation.* New York: Oxford University Press.

Pepper, S. 1942. *World hypotheses.* Berkeley: University of California Press.

Peters, T. 1988. *The leadership alliance.* Des Plaines, IL: Video Publishing House.

Pickering, A. 1995. *The mangle of practice: Time, agency, and science.* Chicago: University of Chicago Press.

Pirsig, R. M. 1974. *Zen and the Art of Motorcycle Maintenance.* New York: Bantam Books.

Quinn, R. E. 1988. *Beyond rational management.* San Francisco: Jossey-Bass.

_____. 1996. *Becoming a master manager: A competency framework.* New York: Wiley.

_____, and K. S. Cameron. 1999. *Diagnosing and changing organizational culture: Based on the competing values framework.* Reading, MA: Addison-Wesley.

Ray, D., and H. Bronstein. 1995. *Teaming up: Making the transition to a self-directed team-based organization.* New York: McGraw-Hill.

Reinhardt, R. 2000. Knowledge management: Linking theory with practice. In *Knowledge management: Classic and contemporary works.* Ed. D. Morey et al. Cambridge, MA: MIT Press, 187–221.

Sayre, K. M. 1997. *Belief and knowledge: Mapping the cognitive landscape.* Lanham, MD: Rowan & Littlefield.

Schein, E. 1996. Culture: The missing concept in organization studies. *Administrative Science Quarterly* 41(2):229–40.

Senge, P. M. 1990. *The fifth discipline: The art and practice of the learning organization.* New York: Doubleday.

Shukla, M. 1997. *Competing through knowledge: Building a learning organization.* New Delhi: Sage.

Sparrow, J. 1998. *Knowledge in organizations: Access to thinking at work.* London: Sage.

Stack, J. 1992. *The great game of business*. New York: Currency Books.

Stenmark, M. 1995. *Rationality in science, religion, and everyday life*. Notre Dame, IN: University of Notre Dame.

Stroup, H. 1966. *Bureaucracy in higher education*. New York: Free Press.

Sveiby, K.-E. 2000. Measuring intangibles and intellectual capital. In *Knowledge management: Classic and contemporary works*. Ed. D. Morey et al. Cambridge, MA: MIT Press, 337–53.

Teece, D. J. 1998. Capturing value from knowledge assets: The new economy, markets for know-how, and intangible assets. *California Management Review* (Special issue on knowledge and the firm) 40(3):55–79.

Thompson, V. A. 1961. *Modern organization: A general theory*. New York: Knopf.

Vaill, P. 1996. *Learning as a way of being*. San Francisco: Jossey-Bass.

van der Heijden, K., and C. Eden. 1998. The theory and praxis of reflective learning in strategy making. In *Managerial and organization cognition: Theory, methods and research*. Ed. C. Eden and J. C. Spender. London: Sage, 58–75.

Vogt, J. F., and K. L. Murrell. 1990. *Empowerment in organizations: How to spark exceptional performance*. San Diego: University Associates.

Wainwright Industries. 1997. *Sincere trust and belief in people: The Wainwright story*. Videotape. St. Peters, MO: Just Learning.

Wheatley, M. J. 1992. *Leadership and the new science: Learning about organization from an orderly universe*. San Francisco: Berrett-Koehler.

Yeung, A. K., et al. 1999. *Organizational learning capacity: Generating and generalizing ideas with impact*. New York: Oxford University Press.

Index

ad hoc teams, 40
alignment: description of, 91–92; forms of, 92

boundaries, 92

change: at conceptual DNA organization, 87, 104; at contextual DNA organization, 87, 104; at factual DNA organization, 86–87, 104; at individual DNA organization, 88, 104; at Johnsonville Sausage, 87; self-assessments, 104; at Springfield Remanufacturing Corporation, 86–87; at Wainwright Industries, 88; at YSI, Inc., 87
clashing of organizations: consortia, 115–117, 122; leadership changes, 112–113, 120–121; mergers, 114–115, 121–122; organizational decline, 118–119, 123; partnerships, 115–117, 122; scenarios, 120–123
codified knowledge, 138
communication, 28–29
compensation: at conceptual DNA organization, 74–75, 95, 101; at contextual DNA organization, 76, 95, 101; at factual DNA organization, 74, 95, 101; at individual DNA organization, 76, 95, 102; at Johnsonville Sausage, 13, 74–75; self-assessments, 101–102; at Springfield Remanufacturing Corporation, 74, 95; at Wainwright Industries, 40, 76; at YSI, Inc., 76
conceptual DNA organization: change at, 87, 104; compensation at, 74–75, 95, 101; contextual DNA organization partnered with, 116; decision making at, 83, 95, 103; employee training/development at, 77–78, 80, 95, 102; factual DNA organization acquisition of, 115, 121–122; governance structure, 55–56, 94, 97; hiring at, 72–73, 95, 101; interpersonal relationships at, 84–85, 103; Johnsonville Sausage case study of, 11–20; leadership style at, 57–58, 94, 98; learning

at, 131–132; mission purpose, 52–53, 94, 97; performance management at, 67, 100; planning at, 62, 94, 99; profits, 89, 95, 105; at Springfield Remanufacturing Corporation, 10; teamwork at, 63–64, 99
consortia: contextual and conceptual organizations, 116; description of, 115–117, 122; factual and contextual organizations, 117, 122
contextual DNA organization: change at, 87, 104; compensation at, 76, 95, 101; conceptual DNA organization partnered with, 116; decision making at, 83, 103; decline of, 118–119, 123; employee training/development at, 78, 80, 95, 102; factual DNA organization merged with, 114–115, 121–122; governance structure, 56, 97; hiring at, 73, 95, 101; interpersonal relationships at, 84–85, 95, 104; leadership style at, 57–58, 94, 98; learning at, 132–134; mission purpose, 53, 94, 97; performance management at, 67–68, 94, 100; planning at, 62, 63, 94, 99; profits, 89, 95, 105; Springfield Remanufacturing Corporation, 10; team-oriented approach, 128; teamwork at, 64–65, 94, 100; YSI case study of, 23–32
continuous improvement program, 36–37
"critical numbers," 4
customer satisfaction index, 37
Cycle of Events model of organizational learning, 137–138

decision making: at conceptual DNA organization, 83, 95, 103; at contextual DNA organization, 83, 95, 103; at factual DNA organization, 81–83, 95, 103; at individual DNA organization, 83, 95, 103; at Johnsonville Sausage, 83; self-assessments, 103; at Springfield Remanufacturing Corporation, 81–83; at Wainwright Industries, 83; at YSI, Inc., 24, 83
discovered knowledge, 138

145

employees: business education of, 7–8; at conceptual DNA organization, 77–78, 80, 102; at contextual DNA organization, 78, 80, 102; at factual DNA organization, 76–77, 80, 102; financial rewards for, 9; hiring of, 30; at individual DNA organization, 78–80, 102; interpersonal conflicts, 31–32; at Johnsonville Sausage, 77–78; orientation of, 30–31; performance development plan, 38; performance measurement of, 31; personal responsibility of, 8–9; satisfaction of, 36; self-assessments, 102; at Springfield Remanufacturing Corporation, 76–77; training/development of, 76–79, 102; at Wainwright Industries, 78–79; at YSI, Inc., 78
employee stock ownership plan, 9, 24
empowerment resources, 127–128

factual DNA organization: change at, 86–87, 104; compensation at, 74, 95, 102; conceptual DNA organization acquired by, 115, 121–122; contextual DNA organization merged with, 114–115, 121–122; decision making at, 81–83, 103; employee training/development at, 76–77, 80, 95, 102; governance structure, 55, 94, 97; hiring at, 71–72, 95, 101; interpersonal relationships at, 84–85, 104; at Johnsonville Sausage, 21; leadership style at, 57, 94, 98, 113, 121; learning, 130–131; mission purpose, 52, 94, 97; performance management at, 65–67, 100; planning at, 61–62, 99; profits, 89, 104; Springfield Remanufacturing Corporation case study of, 3–10; teamwork at, 63, 99; at Wainwright Industries, 42; at YSI, Inc., 32
financial rewards, 9

governance structure: at conceptual DNA organization, 55–56, 94, 97; at contextual DNA organization, 56, 94, 97; at factual DNA organization, 55, 94, 97; at individual DNA organization, 56, 94, 98; at Johnsonville Sausage, 55–56; at Springfield Remanufactur-

ing Corporation, 7, 55; at Wainwright Industries, 56; at YSI, Inc., 56

hiring: at conceptual DNA organization, 72–73, 95, 101; at contextual DNA organization, 73, 95, 101; at factual DNA organization, 71–72, 95, 101; at individual DNA organization, 73, 95, 101; at Johnsonville Sausage, 72–73; self-assessments, 101; at Springfield Remanufacturing Corporation, 71–72; at Wainwright Industries, 73; at YSI, Inc., 73
human resources: compensation, 74–76, 95; employee training/development, 76–79, 95; hiring, 71–73, 95

individual DNA organization: change at, 88, 104; compensation at, 76, 95, 102; decision making at, 83, 103; employee training/development at, 78–80, 95, 102; governance structure, 56, 94, 98; hiring at, 73, 95, 101; interpersonal relationships at, 84–85, 95, 104; leadership style at, 57–58, 98, 112; learning at, 134–135; maturation of, 118, 122–123; mission purpose, 53–54, 94, 97; performance management at, 68, 94, 100; planning at, 63, 94, 99; profits, 89, 95, 105; at Springfield Remanufacturing Corporation, 10; teamwork at, 65, 94, 100; Wainwright Industries case study of, 33–42
interactive stabilization, 92
interpersonal relationships, 84–85, 95, 104–105
invisible knowledge, 138

Johnsonville Sausage: change at, 87; compensation at, 13, 74–75; contract, 19; decision making at, 83; description of, 11; DNA types at, 46; employee training/development at, 13, 77–78, 127; feedback systems at, 20; governance structure at, 55–56; hiring at, 72–73; individual learning at, 15–16; internal customer needs, 19; interpersonal relationships at, 84–85; leadership style at, 57–58; mission